A Guide to International Economics

A Guide to International Economics

Shahruz Mohtadi

BEP BUSINESS EXPERT PRESS

A Guide to International Economics
Copyright © Business Expert Press, LLC, 2019.

First published in 2019 by
Business Expert Press, LLC
222 East 46th Street, New York, NY 10017
www.businessexpertpress.com

ISBN-13: 978-1-63157-439-9 (paperback)
ISBN-13: 978-1-63157-440-5 (e-book)

Business Expert Press Economics and Public Policy Collection

Collection ISSN: 2163-761X (print)
Collection ISSN: 2163-7628 (electronic)

Cover and interior design by S4Carlisle Publishing Services Private Ltd., Chennai, India

First edition: 2019

10 9 8 7 6 5 4 3 2 1

Printed in the United States of America.

Dedication

To Farjam, Sana, and Mona

Abstract

The study of international economics has never been more vital than it is today. The global financial crisis, the economic turmoil in many advanced countries, increasing barriers to international trade, and currency crises have created challenges for both policy makers and corporate decision makers involved in international trade and finance. Corporate managers and MBA students must learn the complex interrelationships between trade policies, the actions of central banks, and changes in government spending and taxes, on interest rates, prices, exchange rates, and economic activity.

This book aims to present a concise introduction to international economics. Unlike standard textbooks on international economics that focus on developing complex theories and models, this book provides a rigorous and lucid approach to the understanding of international trade and finance. It explains the basis and pattern of trade, the effects of trade and trade policies on companies, national welfare, and the global economy. It explains the determination of exchange rates and changes in exchange rates. Finally, it examines the role and impact of national economic policies on the domestic economy and the rest of the world.

This book is suitable for students taking an introductory course in international economics in MBA and other graduate international business programs, and for business practitioners and decision makers with limited knowledge of basic economic principles.

Keywords

comparative advantage; global supply chain; offshoring; tariffs; quotas; subsidies; dumping; World Trade Organization; balance of payments; foreign exchange market; exchange rates; purchasing power parity; arbitrage; aggregate demand; unemployment; inflation; fiscal policy; monetary policy; currency union; currency wars

Contents

Preface

I have been teaching courses in international economics for over 35 years at both the undergraduate and graduate levels. A common complaint of business students is that the traditional textbooks in international economics rely too much on graphs and mathematical formulas to explain complex economic theories and concepts. Another complaint is the relevance and applicability of these models and theories to business decision making and strategic planning. This book aims to provide a basic understanding of international economics without reliance on graphs and equations to explain economic models. It is written for an audience without any extensive knowledge of basic economics and is particularly appropriate for students majoring in business administration, or corporate decision makers.

Acknowledgments

I am indebted to Sana Mohtadi for reviewing a draft of the book and Professor Phillip J. Romero for his helpful recommendations.

Introduction

A Guide to International Economics is divided into two parts: The first part is the theory of international trade and trade policy. It focuses on why nations trade with each other and the basis of trade. It then examines the effects of trade on the domestic economy. There is a consensus that a country will gain from international trade; yet, within the country, some groups will gain, while others will lose. Concerns about the effects of trade on the distribution of income lead governments to enact trade policies aimed at protecting industries and workers that are hurt due to import competition, and other policies aimed at promoting exports. From a business perspective, some domestic companies will face competition from foreign companies, while some other companies will see an opportunity in sales in other countries. International trade creates threats and opportunities for all firms. It becomes vital for corporate managers to gain a fundamental knowledge of the basis and the pattern of trade. They also need to understand the implications of national trade policies and international trade agreements on their costs, revenues, and profits.

The second part of *A Guide to International Economics* is international finance. It focuses on the foreign exchange market and the determination of exchange rates. Managers and corporate decision makers need to understand the impact of changes in exchange rates on the prices of their goods and how to manage exchange rate risk. Open economy macroeconomics focuses on the determination of the level of national output and the price level. It further examines the role of changes in the supply of money, taxes, and government spending on interest rates, exchange rates, national output, and the price level. Companies that operate globally, importing raw materials from other countries, producing parts of their products in other nations, and competing in the global market, must understand the impact of these changes on their operations.

PART I

International Trade Theory

International trade has grown steadily over the past 300 years, although it declined during the Great Depression and between World Wars I and II. From 1945 to 1980, international trade grew faster than ever before due to decreases in trade barriers during the Great Depression and the two wars, and the significant decline in transportation costs. During this period, developing countries primarily exported agricultural goods and commodities to the advanced industrialized countries and imported manufactured products. Beginning in the 1980s, many emerging economies like China, India, and Brazil began to liberalize their trade policies and actively entered the global markets. China became a major exporter of textiles and apparel, and other countries such as Malaysia, Turkey, Mexico, South Korea, Indonesia, and Thailand moved into manufacturing trade. Multinational corporations began to establish subsidiaries and moved some of their production activities to these countries. American companies first moved the production of apparel, shoes, and toys to developing countries, followed by the assembly of cars and electronic goods, to take advantage of lower less-skilled labor costs. Today many companies rely on foreign sources for high-skilled activities, such as programming, software development, chip design, and financial analysis.

Currently, according to the World Trade Organization (WTO), the top exporter of agricultural products is the European Union (EU), comprising 38 percent of global exports, followed by the United States, Brazil, China, and Canada. The EU is also the top exporter of fuels, mining products, and cars. The EU, China, Japan, and South Korea are the principal exporters of steel and iron. China is the world's largest exporter of office and telecommunication equipment, textiles, and clothing. The EU is the leading exporter of cars, followed by Japan, the United States, and

Canada. A major portion of global trade is in services, which includes transportation, travel, communications, construction, insurance, financial, computer and information technologies, and other business services such as operational leasing, technical and professional services, and cultural and recreational services. The United States, the United Kingdom, China, Germany, and Japan are the largest exporters of these services.[1]

---

[1]https://www.wto.org/english/res_e/statis_e/wts2016_e/wts16_toc_e.htm. (accessed June 21, 2017)

CHAPTER 1

The Basics of a Market: Supply and Demand and Equilibrium

To understand the basis for international trade, we need to explain how the price of a product is determined and why does the price change. Every product or service has a market composed of producers (suppliers) and consumers (demanders) of the product. The interaction of the suppliers and demanders determines the price and the quantity sold of a product.

Demand

To have a demand for a product, a consumer must want the product, can afford to buy the product, and finally has plans to purchase the product. Holding other variables constant, the most important determinant of the quantity demanded of a product is the price of the product. As the price of a product rises, a consumer will be less willing to buy the product and will look to buy an alternative product that is less expensive. Conversely, as the price of the product falls, a consumer will be more willing to buy the product as opposed to the more expensive alternative. This is expressed as *the law of demand* which states: holding everything else constant, an increase in the price of a product leads to a decrease in the quantity demanded of the product, and a decrease in the price of a product leads to an increase in the quantity demanded of the product. Table 1.1 is a representative demand schedule for a product.

To arrive at the market demand for the product we add all the individual demands for the product. In addition to the price, there are other determinants that affect the demand for a product. These include tastes and preferences, income, the price of other goods, number of buyers,

Table 1.1 Demand Schedule

Price ($)	Quantity Demanded
7	0
6	10
5	20
4	30
3	40
2	50
1	60

and expected future prices. Any changes in these variables will result in a change in the demand for the product. For example, if people's income increases, they will be able to afford to buy more of a product, so the demand for the product will increase. If a product has a close substitute, then a rise in the price of a substitutable product will increase the demand for the product. For example, if the price of Pepsi Cola increases, the quantity demanded of Pepsi Cola decreases, and the demand for Coca Cola increases. If a product has a complement, then a rise in the price of a complement will decrease the demand for the product. For example, if the price of printers increases, the quantity demanded of printers decreases, and the demand for ink cartridges decreases. If consumers' tastes and preferences for a product change, then the demand for the product will change. For example, if studies show that consuming diet sodas increases the chance of liver cancer, then the demand for diet sodas will decrease. Changes in the number of buyers also results in a change in the demand for a product. An increase in the number of buyers increases the market demand, while a decrease in the number of buyers decreases the market demand. Finally, changes in expected prices in the future affect the current demand for the product. If consumers expect a decrease in the price of a product in the future, they will postpone their purchases today, leading to a decrease in the current demand for the product and vice versa.

Supply

A producer must be able and willing to produce a good if it is profitable. The most important determinant of the quantity supplied of a product is the price of the product. As the price of a product rises, holding the cost of producing the product constant, the greater the potential for profits, which leads a firm to produce more of the product and vice versa. This is summarized in *the law of supply*: holding everything else constant, an increase in the price of a product leads to an increase in the quantity supplied of the product and a decrease in the price of a product leads to a decrease in the quantity supplied of the product. Table 1.2 is an example of the supply schedule of a product.

Table 1.2 *Supply schedule*

Price ($)	Quantity Supplied
7	60
6	50
5	40
4	30
3	20
2	10
1	0

In addition to the price of the product, other variables affect the supply of a product. These include the price of inputs, changes in technology, the price of related goods, expected future prices, taxes, subsidies, government regulations, and the number of suppliers. Changes in input prices will change the supply of a product. For example, if the price of steel in car manufacturing rises, then the cost of car production increases and a car company will decrease the supply of cars. Changes in technology that result in a decrease in production costs will increase the supply of a product. Changes in the price of related goods will also change the supply. If Ford Motor Company observes that the price of SUVs has risen relative to sedans, it will increase the quantity supplied of SUVs and decrease the supply of sedans. Changes in expected price in the future will affect supply. If a company expects a higher price in the future, it will withhold the supply of the product today to take advantage of higher prices in the future. Companies consider business taxes as costs, so if taxes increase, then supply decreases.

Conversely, a subsidy is a direct payment to companies by the government, so an increase in production subsidies leads to an increase in supply. Government business regulations that lead to higher costs decrease the supply. Finally, an increase in the number of producers leads to an increase in market supply.

Market Equilibrium

Let us examine how the suppliers and demanders interact with each other in the market using the data in Table 1.3.

Table 1.3 Market equilibrium

Price ($)	Quantity demanded	Quantity supplied	Result	Price change
7	0	60	Surplus	Decrease
6	10	50	Surplus	Decrease
5	20	40	Surplus	Decrease
4	30	30	Equilibrium	None
3	40	20	Shortage	Increase
2	50	10	Shortage	Increase
1	60	0	Shortage	Increase

At a price of six dollars, the quantity demanded is equal to 10 and the quantity supplied is equal to 50. In other words, the producers are willing to supply a larger quantity than consumers are willing to purchase, resulting in a surplus or excess supply of the product. To reduce this excess supply of the product, the firms will lower the price. If the suppliers lower the price to five dollars, the quantity demanded increases to 20, but there will still be a surplus of 20 units, which puts pressure on the suppliers to further reduce the price. The price will continue to decrease until the quantity demanded equals the quantity supplied.

At a price of two dollars, the quantity demanded is equal to 50, while the quantity supplied is equal to 10. That is, consumers are willing to purchase a larger quantity of the product than producers are willing to supply, resulting in a shortage or excess demand for the product. Because of this shortage, some consumers will be willing to pay a higher price for the product. If the price rises to three dollars, the quantity supplied will increase to 20, but there will still be a shortage of the product. The price will continue to increase until the quantity supplied equals the quantity demanded.

At the price of four dollars, the quantity demanded is equal to 30, which is also equal to the quantity supplied, and the market will be in equilibrium, which means there is neither a shortage nor a surplus, and thus no pressure for the price to change.

Changes in supply or demand will move the market out of equilibrium, creating either a shortage or a surplus, which leads to changes in a new equilibrium price and quantity of the product. An increase in demand with no change in supply leads to a shortage and a rise in price and quantity, while a decrease in demand with no change in supply leads to a surplus and a fall in price and quantity. An increase in supply with no change in demand leads to a surplus and a decline in price and a rise in quantity, while a decrease in supply with no change in demand leads to a shortage and a rise in price and a decline in quantity.

Suppose the equilibrium domestic price of the product is four dollars, but the world price is two dollars. The consumers in the domestic market will prefer to purchase the product at the lower world price. The domestic suppliers will then be forced to lower their price to two dollars. The decrease in the price of the product leads to an increase in the quantity demanded to 50 and a decrease in the quantity supplied to 10. The shortage will be supplied by imports of 40 units.

But now let the world price be six dollars, meaning the rest of the world is willing to pay a higher price for the product. The domestic producers will then increase the quantity supplied to 50 units. This increase in the price will decrease the quantity demanded to 10. The resulting surplus of 40 units will then be exported.

Thus, the difference between the domestic price and the world price of a product is the basis for imports and exports. A product is imported if the international price is lower than the domestic price, and it is exported if the international price is higher than the domestic price.

CHAPTER 2

The Basis for Trade: Absolute Advantage and Comparative Advantage

Mercantilism

During the seventeenth and eighteenth centuries, *mercantilism* was the dominant doctrine of international trade. According to this doctrine, a country's wealth was measured in terms of its holding of gold and silver. Mercantilists believed that exports would lead to inflows of gold and silver, and imports would lead to outflows of these precious metals. Thus, to increase a nation's wealth, the country should increase its exports and decrease its imports. Mercantilists viewed trade as a zero-sum game, in which one country's gain was at the expense of another country. Based on this mercantilist doctrine, governments placed a variety of taxes and restrictions on imports and provided incentives and funding to encourage exports. Governments also gave exclusive rights to individual companies to engage in trade. These trade monopolies like the Hudson Bay Company and the Dutch East India Trading Company generated high profits, which, in turn, contributed to the wealth of the rulers.

Today, a different kind of mercantilism has emerged, where the accumulation of gold is replaced with jobs. The so-called neo-mercantilists believe that exports generate jobs and imports destroy domestic jobs. So, a trade surplus will increase the number of jobs and national income. Like the mercantilists, they view free trade as a zero-sum game and lobby the government to enact policies that aggressively promote exports and limit imports.

In the late eighteenth and early nineteenth centuries, some philosophers and political economists, such as David Hume, Adam Smith, and

David Ricardo, began to criticize the doctrine of mercantilism. Hume argued that a trade surplus and the accumulation of gold and silver increased the nation's money supply. The increase in the money supply would then lead to an increase in the prices of goods. The higher prices of goods would make exports more expensive and imports cheaper, leading to a decline in exports and a rise in imports, and the elimination of the trade surplus.

Adam Smith and the Theory of Absolute Advantage

Adam Smith was a Scottish philosopher and political economist who, in 1776, published his now famous book, *An Inquiry into the Nature and Causes of the Wealth of Nations*. In Book IV, he criticizes mercantilism and maintains that the wealth of a nation does not increase by accumulating gold and silver, but rather by the number of goods and services available for consumption through trade. In his words,

> If a foreign country can supply us with a commodity cheaper than we ourselves can make it, better buy it of them with some part of the produce of our own industry, employed in a way in which we have some advantage.[1]

Smith maintained that each country has an *absolute advantage* in the production of a product, that is, if a worker can produce more units of a product than another country. Then each country can specialize in the production of that product and exchange it with the product that it has a comparative disadvantage.

To illustrate trade based on absolute advantage, let us assume there are two countries, Home and Foreign, and two products, shirts and computers. The average worker in Home can produce nine shirts or five computers in an hour, while the average worker in Foreign can produce four shirts or seven computers in an hour. Comparing the labor productivities in each country, we can observe that the worker at Home is more productive in producing shirts and the Foreign worker is more productive

---

[1] A. Smith. 1937. *An Inquiry into the Nature and Causes of the Wealth of Nations* (New York, NY: The Modern Library/Random House), p. 424.

in producing computers. Thus, Home has an absolute advantage in shirt production and Foreign in computer production. Let us assume that both countries have 10 workers and each country devotes half of its workers to shirt production and the other half to computer production. Each country produces and consumes the combination of goods in Table 2.1.

Table 2.1 Production possibilities

	Home	Foreign	Total
Computers	25	35	60
Shirts	45	20	65

According to Smith, each country should then completely specialize in the production of the product on which it has an absolute advantage, as represented in Table 2.2.

Table 2.2 Production possibilities after specialization

	Home	Foreign	Total
Computers	0	70	70
Shirts	90	0	90

Notice that after specialization, there is an increase in the total world production of both products, which is referred to as production gains in specialization. Whether or not the two countries will trade with each other will depend on the *terms of trade*, defined as the amount of imports a country can trade for its exports. Suppose the two countries agree to a terms of trade of one shirt for one computer. Let Home keep 60 shirts for domestic consumption. It can then export 30 shirts and import 30 computers. Similarly, let Foreign keep 40 computers for domestic consumption. It can then export 30 computers and import 30 shirts. Table 2.3 shows the consumption of the two products after specialization and trade.

Table 2.3 Consumption possibilities after trade

	Home	Foreign
Computers	30	40
Shirts	60	30

Notice that after trade, Home gains 5 extra computers and 15 extra shirts, while Foreign gains 5 extra computers and 10 extra shirts, which are referred to as consumption gains from trade.

David Ricardo and the Theory of Comparative Advantage

Now suppose the average worker in Home can produce eight shirts or four computers per hour, while in the Foreign country, the average worker can produce four shirts or three computers per hour. In this case, Home's workers have an absolute advantage in the production of both goods. Would Home then trade with Foreign? In 1800, David Ricardo, a wealthy English businessman, read the *Wealth of Nations* and posed the same question. In his book *Principles of Political Economy and Taxation* he wrote,

> It will appear . . . that a country possessing very considerable advantages in machinery and skill, and which may, therefore, be enabled to manufacture commodities with much less labour than her neighbors, may, in return for such commodities, import a portion of its corn required for it consumption, even if its land were more fertile, and corn could be grown with less labour than in a country from which it was imported.[2]

Ricardo demonstrated that mutually beneficial trade is still possible if instead of comparing productivities across countries, we compare the *opportunity costs* of producing each product in each country. Opportunity cost is the amount of a unit of product X that must be given up in order to produce a unit of product Y. If a country can produce a product at a lower opportunity cost, then it has a *comparative advantage* in the production of that product. Ricardo relied on the labor theory of value and used the example of England and Portugal, and wine and cloth to explain the law of comparative advantage. In his own words,

---

[2]D. Ricardo. 1957. *On the Principles of Political Economy and Taxation* (London: J.M. Dent & Sons), p. 83.

To produce the wine in Portugal, might require only the labour of 80 men for one year, and to produce the cloth in the same country, might require the labour of 90 men for the same time. It would, therefore, be advantageous for her to export wine in exchange for cloth. This exchange might even take place, notwithstanding that the commodity imported by Portugal could be produced there with less labour than in England. Though she could make the cloth with the labour of 90 men, she would import it from a country where it required the labour of 100 men to produce it, because it would be advantageous to her rather to employ her capital in the production of wine, for which she would obtain more cloth from England, than she could produce by diverting a portion of her capital from the cultivation of vines to the manufacture of cloth.[3]

Ricardo's insights are used to construct a model based on the following assumptions:

1. There are only two countries and two products.
2. Labor is the only factor of production, and each country has a fixed amount of labor that is fully employed.
3. Labor can work in both industries and can easily move between industries.
4. Countries may have different technologies, but firms in each country use the same technology to produce the two products.
5. There are constant returns to scale, which means that an increase in the number of workers by a certain percentage leads to an equal percentage increase in the level of output.
6. There is perfect competition in the market, which means there are many small-sized firms producing an identical product. The price of the product is equal to the extra cost of hiring the labor.
7. There are no barriers to trade and no transportation costs.

---

[3]D. Ricardo. 1957. *On the Principles of Political Economy and Taxation* (London: J. M. Dent & Sons), p. 82.

So, in our example, for Home to produce eight shirts it must give up four computers, which means the opportunity cost of producing one shirt is a half computer. Similarly, to produce four computers, it must give up eight shirts, which means the opportunity cost of one computer is two shirts. In Foreign, the opportunity cost of producing one computer is 4/3 shirts, and the opportunity cost of producing one shirt is 3/4 computers. We can see that Home can produce shirts at a lower opportunity cost, and Foreign can produce computers at a lower opportunity cost. Home has a comparative advantage in shirt production and Foreign in computer production. With 10 workers, let both countries produce and consume the combination in Table 2.4.

Table 2.4 Production and consumption possibilities before trade

	Home	Foreign	Total
Computers	16	9	25
Shirts	48	28	76

Whether the countries will trade with each other depends on the terms of trade. Home will export shirts only if it can get a price of more than a half of a computer, and it will import computers if the price is less than two shirts. Foreign will export computers if it can get a price of more than 4/3 shirts, and it will import shirts if it can pay a price of less than 3/4 computers. Let the international terms of trade be equal to one computer for 5/3 shirts, which is between each country's domestic relative price of the computer. Home will then use all its 10 workers to produce 80 shirts and will give up the production of computers, while Foreign will completely specialize and produce 30 computers.

If Home decides to consume 50 shirts, it can then export the remaining 30 shirts and import 18 computers. Similarly, if Foreign decides to consume 12 computers, it can then export 18 computers and import 30 shirts as shown in Table 2.5.

Table 2.5 Consumption after trade

	Home	Foreign	Total
Computers	18	12	30
Shirts	50	30	80

Notice that Home gains two extra computers and two extra shirts, while Foreign gains three extra computers and two extra shirts.

To see an application of absolute and comparative advantage, we can look at the data for the U.S. textile, apparel, and wheat industries.[4] In 2014, the average sale per employee for all American apparel producers was $70,000, while for the textile industry, producing the fabric and material inputs for apparel was even more productive, with annual sales per employee of $232,000. In comparison, the average employee in China had sales per year in the apparel industry of $27,000 and $20,000 in the textile industry Thus, a worker in the United States produced $70,000/$27,000 = 2.6 times more apparel sales than a worker in China, and $232,000/$20,000 = 12 times more in textile sales. In the wheat industry, the typical farm in the United States grew more than 10,000 bushels of wheat per worker, while in China a typical farm produced only 300 bushels per worker, so the U.S. farm was 10,000/300 = 33 times more productive. Thus, the United States has an absolute advantage in the textile, apparel, and wheat industries. Then, how do we explain the fact that the United States imports textiles and apparel from China and exports wheat to China?

Let's look at the opportunity costs of producing apparel, textiles, and wheat in each country. In the United States, the opportunity cost of apparel is 10,000/$70,000 = 0.14 bushels of wheat, while the opportunity cost of textiles is 10,000/$232,000 = 0.07 bushels. In China, the opportunity cost of apparel is 300/$20,000 = 0.013, and the opportunity cost of textiles is 300/$27,000 = 0.011. Thus, China has a lower opportunity cost in producing both textiles and apparel than the United States. Similarly, in the United States, the opportunity cost of wheat in terms of textiles is $232,000/10,000 = 23.2, and the opportunity cost of wheat in terms of apparel is $70,000/10,000 = 7.0, while in China the opportunity cost of wheat in terms of textiles is $20,000/300 = 66.7, and the opportunity cost of wheat in terms of apparel is $27,000/300 = 90.

---

[4]These data are from R.C. Feenstra and A.M. Taylor. 2017. *International Economics*. 4th ed., Table 2.2, p. 41, actual data for U.S. apparel and textile data are from U.S. Bureau Labor Statistics, U.S. wheat data are from USDA Wheat Yearbook, 2014. All Chinese data are from China Statistical Yearbook 2013.

Therefore, the United States has a lower opportunity cost of producing wheat. This illustrates why the United States exports wheat and imports textiles and apparel from China, as predicted by the Ricardian model.

The Heckscher–Ohlin Model

Smith and Ricardo simply assumed that comparative advantage was due to different labor productivities yet did not explain the causes of comparative advantage. In the early 1930s two economists, Eli Heckscher and Bertil Ohlin, developed a new model that explained comparative advantage.

The Heckscher–Ohlin (H-O) model has the following assumptions:

1. There are two factors of production, labor and capital. Each country has a fixed endowment or supply of labor and capital. The supply of labor is measured as the total number of workers in a country, and the supply of capital is measured as the total number of machines or the total value of the capital goods. A country will be relatively labor-abundant if the ratio of the total number of workers relative to the total number of machines is greater than that of another country. Notice that it is the ratio of labor to capital that determines factor abundance, not the absolute number. For example, the United States has more workers and capital than Switzerland, yet Switzerland has a higher capital-to-labor ratio than the United States and therefore is the capital-abundant country.

2. There are two products. The products are classified based on their factor intensities. If a product requires more workers relative to machines, then the product is labor-intensive, and if the product requires more machines relative to workers, then it is capital-intensive. Again, it is important to note that factor intensity is based on the ratio of capital to labor used in producing a product.

3. The two products are produced in perfectly competitive markets. The firms are price takers, which means that the market sets the price of the product and a firm cannot influence the price.

4. Both countries have access to the same technology in producing the two products. This is a departure from the Ricardian model, which assumed different technologies.

5. There are constant returns to scale.

6. Capital and labor cannot move between countries but can move between industries within the country. Workers are qualified to work in both industries, and wages are the same in both industries. For example, if the shirt industry pays a higher wage than the computer industry, workers will leave the computer industry to work in the shirt industry. The increase in the supply of workers in the shirt industry will lower the wages in the shirt industry, and the decrease in the supply of workers in the computer industry will raise the wages in the computer industry. This process continues until wages in both industries are equal to each other. Similarly, machines can be used in both industries, and the price of capital referred to as the rental price of capital will be equal in both industries.

7. There are no barriers to free trade and no transportation costs.

8. Tastes in the two countries are identical, which means that if faced with the same relative price ratio and the same level of national income, each country will consume the same proportion of the two products.

Based on these assumptions, a labor-abundant country will tend to have lower wages relative to capital rents and a capital-abundant country will have lower capital rents relative to wages. Therefore, a labor-abundant country can produce the labor-intensive product at a lower cost, and a capital-abundant country can produce the capital-intensive product at a lower cost. In other words, a labor-abundant country will have a comparative advantage and will export the labor-intensive product and import the capital-intensive product, and a capital-abundant country will have a comparative advantage in the capital-intensive product and will export the product and import the labor-intensive product.

Suppose Home is the labor-abundant country and shirts are labor-intensive, and Foreign is the capital-abundant country and computers are capital-intensive. Then, according to this theorem, Home will have a comparative advantage in shirt production and Foreign will have a comparative advantage in computer production. If the international terms of trade lie between the two countries' domestic relative prices, then Home will increase its production of shirts and export shirts and Foreign will increase its production of computers and will export computers.

Similar to the Ricardian model, Home will import computers and Foreign will import shirts. International trade permits each country to consume a combination of the two products beyond what each country could produce without trade.

When Home increases the production of shirts, the opportunity cost and the price of shirts increase, and the price of computers decreases due to lower import prices. As Foreign increases the production of computers, the opportunity cost and the price of computers increase, and the price of shirts decreases due to lower Home import price. This will continue until the relative prices of the products in both countries equal the international terms of trade.

The H-O theorem implies that high-income countries like the United States and Japan, which are capital-abundant, will be exporters of relatively capital-intensive products, such as machinery, precision equipment, and chemicals, while lower-middle-income countries like Bangladesh and Vietnam, which are labor-abundant, will be exporters of labor-intensive products, such as clothing, toys, and sports equipment.

There have been many empirical tests of the H-O theory with mixed results, particularly using the two-country two-factor model. One reason is that the model assumes the same technologies and tastes in the countries and ignores the presence of trade barriers and transportation costs. Another reason is that it is difficult to measure the relative supplies of factors of production and relative factor intensities of products.

The Effect of Trade on Income Distribution

Let us examine how trade affects the domestic industries and the incomes of the factors of production. To do so, we must explain how wages and capital rents are determined. A firm will employ a factor of production up to the point where the value produced by using an additional unit of the factor, referred to as the value of the marginal product of the factor, is equal to the cost of hiring that factor. The value of the marginal product of a factor is equal to the marginal product of that factor, which is measured as the increase in output due to hiring an extra unit of the factor, multiplied by the price of the output. The cost of labor is the wage rate, and the cost of capital is the rental price of capital.

As explained earlier, with trade the export industry expands and the import-competing industry contracts. At Home, the production of shirts increases, and the production of computers decreases. Since shirts are labor-intensive, the increase in the production of shirts leads to a substantial increase in the demand for workers. On the other hand, since computers are capital-intensive, the decrease in the production of computers leads to a small decrease in the demand for workers. Since labor can move between the two industries, the relatively small number of workers released from the computer industry will move to work in the shirt industry. However, the shirt industry needs more workers than those coming from the computer industry. This causes a shortage of workers, leading to an increase in wages in both industries.

In the computer industry, the production of computers decreases, and since computers are capital-intensive, there will be a large decrease in the demand for capital in the computer industry. In the shirt industry, the production of shirts increases, and since shirts are labor-intensive, there will be a small increase in the demand for capital. Thus, the increase in the supply of capital released from the computer industry will be higher than the increase in the demand for capital in the shirt industry, leading to a decrease in capital rents.

We have concluded that at Home the price of shirts increases, the price of computers decreases, and wages increase in both industries. So are the workers better off after trade? The workers who spend most of their incomes on buying computers are better off since their wages have increased and the price of computers has decreased. What about the workers who spend most of their incomes on buying shirts, whose price has risen? Two economists, Wolfgang Stolper and Paul Samuelson, developed a theory that demonstrated that with trade, the real income of the abundant factor rises, and the real income of the scarce factor falls.[5] According to this theorem, the percentage change in the income of a factor of production will be higher than the percentage change in the price of the product that uses that factor intensively. For example, at Home, if after trade, the price of shirts increases by 5 percent, then wages will increase by

---

[5]W.F. Stolper and P.A. Samuelson. November, 1941. "Protection and Real Wages." *The Review of Economic Studies* 9, no. 1, pp. 58–73.

more than 5 percent. Similarly, if price of computers falls by 10 percent, the income of capital owners falls by more than 10 percent. So, at Home, workers gain and owners of capital lose, regardless of whether they produce shirts or computers.

The Stolper–Samuelson theorem suggests that even though a country gains from free trade, within the country, some factors gain while other factors lose. Therefore, at Home, labor will be in favor of free trade, while capital owners will be against free trade. Applying this to the U.S. economy, the H-O theorem suggests that since the United States is abundant in high-skilled labor, it will have a comparative advantage in high-skilled-intensive products. It will then export products that require a relatively large quantity of skilled workers and import products that require a relatively large supply of unskilled workers. The result is a decrease in the wages of the unskilled workers and an increase in the wages of the skilled workers.

The Specific Factor Model

One of the assumptions of the Stolper–Samuelson theorem is that in the long run, both labor and capital can move between the two industries. However, in the short run, either labor or capital can be specific to a particular industry and cannot move between the two industries. For example, workers in the computer industry may not have the skills to work in the shirt industry, or the machines used in the shirt industry cannot be used to produce computers.

Suppose workers have the skills to work in both industries but capital is specific, that is, machines used in the shirt industry cannot be used in the computer industry. At Home, with the increase in the price of shirts, workers move from the computer industry to the shirt industry, leading to an increase in the production of shirts and a decrease in the production of computers. Since labor is mobile, and the production of shirts is labor-intensive, there will be a net increase in the demand for labor and an increase in wages in both industries. However, since capital is specific, the increase in the workers makes each additional worker less productive in the shirt industry. This means the percentage increase in wages will be less than the percentage increase in the price of shoes. Whether or not workers gain or lose depends on their consumption patterns. If they spend most of their income on computers, whose price has fallen, they gain, but if the workers spend most of their incomes on shoes, whose price has risen, they lose.

Let us now examine what happens to capital rents in each industry. As more workers move to the shirt industry, the fixed number of machines becomes more productive. The increased productivity of the machines plus the increase in the price of shirts leads to a higher percentage increase in capital rents than the percentage increase in the price of shoes. Similarly, as fewer workers are available in the computer industry, the machines in the computer industry become less productive. This percentage decrease in productivity plus the percentage decrease in the price of computers leads to a higher percentage decrease in capital rents than the percentage decrease in computer prices. So capital owners in the shirt industry gain, while the capital owners in the computer industry lose. So, the specific factors model concludes that the factor of production specific to the export industry gains, while the factor specific to the import-competing industry loses.

CHAPTER 3

New Trade Theories: Economies of Scale, Product Differentiation, and Intra-industry Trade

Trade models based on comparative advantage are due to differences in productivities or factor endowments that explain *inter-industry trade*, which represents trade in products in different industries, like aircraft and apparel, or wheat and oil. However, most of the merchandise trade among industrialized countries is in the form of *intra-industry* trade, which is trade in similar products, like cars for cars, or computers for computers. These countries have the same relative factor endowments, and the traded products have the same factor intensities, so the pattern of trade cannot be explained by the H-O model.

A new set of models known as *New Trade Theory* has been developed to explain this pattern of trade.[1] These models are based on economies of scale and imperfect competition. *Economies of scale* refer to a decrease in average costs, calculated as the total cost of production divided by the total output produced when there is an increase in output or scale of production. There are two kinds of economies of scale: internal and external.

---

[1] P. Krugman. May, 1983m. "New Theories of Trade among Industrial Countries," *American Economic Review* 73, no. 2, pp. 343–347, and E. Helpman. Spring, 1999. "The Structure of Foreign Trade," *Journal of Economic Perspectives* 13, no. 2, pp. 121–144.

External Economies of Scale

External economies of scale occurs when the size of the whole industry gets larger, the firms within the industry enjoy lower average costs. The industry is characterized by many firms clustered within a geographical area. Examples include the semiconductor industry in Silicon Valley, California, the entertainment industry in Hollywood, the banking and finance industry in New York and London, the information services industry in Bangalore, and the apparel industry in several cities in China.

There are several reasons why firms may cluster in a geographic area. First, a group of firms can attract a large number of specialized workers. Workers will be attracted to a city with a large number of firms, as it increases their job prospects. New firms also cluster in and around a city that has a large number of similar firms because they would be able to find the qualified workers easily. Second, a new production technology by a firm can spread to other firms, either formally, through direct contact between firms, or informally, when workers in different companies mix socially and share information about technical issues. Third, this clustering of manufacturing firms also encourages the suppliers of these firms to cluster around the same geographic area. The increased competition among these suppliers leads to lower input costs to the industry.

What determines the location of the industry in a particular area? Often it is a historical event or an accident. For example, in 1895 a teenage girl made a bedspread for her brother's wedding, which eventually led to a carpet-manufacturing industry that supplies more than 85 percent of all carpets sold in the United States and 45 percent of worldwide carpet sales.[2] The American entertainment and movie industry moved to Hollywood, California, in early twentieth century primarily because of the warm weather and extensive sunny days, which allowed the movie production companies to shoot outside and to scout locations within a short distance from Los Angeles that looked like a farm, a factory, a jungle, or snowy peaks. New York City became the financial and banking center of the United States because of international trade. The port of New York

---

[2]http://www.atlasobscura.com/articles/from-the-bedspread-capital-of-the-world-to-the-carpet-capital-of-the-world (accessed July 15, 2017)

was a central location for exports to Europe and proved to be much more convenient than either the ports of Philadelphia or Boston. Furthermore, the Hudson River was much deeper than the Charles River in Boston or the Delaware River in Philadelphia. The construction of the Erie Canal (1817–1825), which connected the Hudson River to the Great Lakes and the American West, and the introduction of the first regularly scheduled transatlantic passenger service added to the importance of New York City.[3]

Internal Economies of Scale

Internal economies of scale refer to the decrease in average costs of a single firm when it increases its level of production. This is because a firm can spread its start-up and overhead costs over larger units of the product. Internal economies of scale lead to a market structure known as *monopolistic competition*. In this market, there are a large number of small firms producing a slightly differentiated product. Since each firm's product is unique relative other firms, it has some control over the price. To remain competitive, the firm will concentrate on increasing its output to take advantage of economies of scale and lower average costs. It is also easy to enter and exit from the market due to economic profits and losses. Consumers prefer product variety and will search for the firm that produces their ideal variety. Two relationships determine the number of firms in the monopolistically competitive market and the prices they charge. First, the higher the number of firms in the market, the more the competition and the lower the price. Second, the higher the number of firms in the market, the smaller the market share and output of each firm and the higher the average cost.

In the short run, if the price is higher than average costs, the firms will be making profits. Over time, this encourages new firms to enter the market producing slightly differentiated products. This increased competition reduces the demand for each firm and lowers the price until it equals the average costs. If the price is less than the average cost, the firms will be

---

[3]Johnston M. "How New York Became the Center of American Finance," *Investopedia*. http://www.investopedia.com/articles/investing/022516/how-new-york-became-center-american-finance.asp#ixzz4nI8Tdis6 (accessed July 16, 2017)

making economic losses, and some firms will leave the industry. In the absence of trade, the size of the domestic market determines the number of firms and the price of the product.

International trade creates an incentive for firms to export their products. A firm that exports will have a larger market and will be able to take advantage of economies of scale and lower average costs. For some domestic firms, there will be an increase in demand for their varieties by consumers in the foreign country. For other domestic firms, the demand for their varieties will decrease due to foreign competition leading to lower sales and higher average costs. If the average costs rise above the price, those firms will suffer losses and will exit the market. The same process occurs in the foreign country. The increased market size due to trade leads to fewer firms in the market, although we cannot predict whether these new firms will be located at home or in the foreign country.

In addition to lower prices, consumers in both countries will enjoy greater varieties of the product. For example, a study of the car industry in the United States indicated that during the period 1972 to 2001, the number of imported varieties of cars in the United States more than tripled, with consumers gaining an average of $1,000 per person due to lower prices.[4]

Outsourcing and Global Supply Chains

Multinational corporations conduct a significant volume of trade through foreign direct investment, outsourcing, and global supply chains. Technological changes, lower transportation costs, lower barriers to trade have contributed to the development and expansion of global supply chains.

Foreign direct investment occurs when a domestic firm purchases a controlling share of a foreign firm, or when a domestic firm builds a new factory in a foreign country. If the factory produces the identical product in the foreign factory, then it is called *horizontal foreign direct investment*. If the factory produces parts of the finished product, then it is referred to as *vertical foreign direct investment*.

---

[4]C. Broda and D. Weinstein. May, 2006. "Globalization and the Gains from Variety," *Quarterly Journal of Economics* 121, no. 2, pp. 541–585.

The primary motivation for vertical foreign direct investment is to lower the overall costs of production. A firm will outsource the production of different components and the final assembly of the product to a location with the lowest cost.

The principal reason for horizontal foreign direct investment is to locate production near a company's primary market in order to minimize trade and transportation costs. For example, Toyota and Hyundai produce a large percentage of their cars in the United States, Canada, and Mexico.

In outsourcing, a firm needs to identify a lineup of all the activities involved in the production, marketing, sales, and service of a product. For example, in manufacturing an iPad, these activities include research; design and engineering; production of components such as display, battery, camera, chipset, and processor; assembly of the final product; and finally marketing and after-sales service. This set of activities is sometimes called the value chain for a product, where each activity adds more to the final value of the product. It is more useful to arrange these activities based on the level of labor skills required in each stage of production. For example, the assembly of an iPad requires the least skilled labor, while design, research, and development require the most skilled labor. Next, the firm will then calculate the ratio of skilled to unskilled workers for each activity. In deciding which activities to outsource, the firm will then compare the domestic relative labor cost of each activity with the relative foreign labor cost. For example, if the labor costs of assembly production are lower in China, then Apple will outsource assembly production to China, and if the labor costs of the display are lower in Taiwan, then it will outsource display production to a Taiwanese company.

In addition to labor costs, a firm must also consider the additional costs of doing business in a foreign country. A country may have poor roads or ports, which increases transportation costs. Alternatively, the country may suffer power outages or may have higher construction and energy costs. In deciding on what activity to outsource, the home company must then weigh the savings from lower labor costs against these other costs.

The development of global supply chains has created new trade patterns as companies in a country specialize in an activity or stage of the production chain based on comparative advantage. Apple's iPhone and iPad are designed in the United States, the iPhone's display is mainly made in Japan and South Korea, while the Touch ID sensor is made in Taiwan. Apple's list of suppliers stretches to more than 200 various suppliers located throughout the world. Apple's devices are mainly assembled in China, which is why we continue to see "Made in China" on most of Apple's products.

Comparative Advantage versus Competitive Advantage

A country's comparative advantage should not be confused with a company's competitive advantage. In the advanced countries, some business executives complain about not being able to compete against companies in countries with lower labor costs, while politicians blame the loss of domestic jobs to low-cost foreign competition and domestic companies moving their operations and jobs to low-wage countries. This confusion is due to misunderstandings of the differences between countries and companies. In the 1980s, Lee Iacocca, the chief executive officer of Chrysler car company, complained that Chrysler was at least as "competitive" as the Japanese car companies, but was still losing market share and, therefore, arguing that competition was "unfair." Based on the theory of comparative advantage, the reason was that Chrysler was not competing against Japanese car companies as much as it opposed to American companies that enjoyed an even higher productivity over their respective Japanese competitors in other products. American car companies might be able to compete with the Japanese companies, but if American farmers are comparatively more productive than Japanese farmers, then the United States would export agricultural products to Japan in exchange for Japanese cars, which was precisely the pattern of trade between the two countries[5] . These days the same arguments have emerged concerning trade with countries like China, South Korea, and other emerging industrialized countries.

Another difference between countries and companies is that companies can go bankrupt, but countries cannot. A company faced with lower-priced imports will be driven out of business and go bankrupt.

---

[5]D.A. Irwin. 1996. *Against the Tide: An Intellectual History of Free Trade* (Princeton, NJ: Princeton University Press), p. 266.

Where an industry may shrink due to trade, another industry will expand in the long run. Finally, outsourcing by firms to gain a competitive advantage is another indicator of the law of comparative advantage at work.[6]

The Gravity Model of Trade

When we examine the global pattern of trade, we observe that the volume of trade is highest among high-income countries and countries that are geographically close to each other. This observation has led to the development of the gravity model of trade. The name is derived from Isaac Newton's law of gravity, which states that the force of gravity between two objects is positively related to the size of the two objects and negatively related to the distance between the objects. The gravity model of international trade suggests that the volume of trade between two countries will be greater the larger the economic sizes of the countries, the shorter the geographic distance between them, and the lower the barriers to trade between them.

A country with a large economy can produce a larger number of varieties of products which can be exported to another country with a similar size economy. This is why 4 of the top 15 trading partners of the United States are Japan, Germany, the United Kingdom, and France, yet the United States' top two trading partners are Mexico and Canada. One primary reason is the geographic proximity of Mexico and Canada, which substantially lowers transportation costs. These gravity models show that a 1 percent increase in the distance between the two countries is associated with a decline of 0.7 to 1 percent in trade.

Trade barriers also significantly affect the volume of trade between countries. One of the most interesting findings of gravity models of trade between the United States and Canada is that even though the two countries have few national barriers to trade, there is much more trade between Canadian provinces than between American states and Canadian provinces. The gravity model has been used to examine other variables that

---

[6]P. Krugman. 1996. "A Country Is Not a Company," *Harvard Business Review*, January-February Issue, pp. 40–51.

affect the volume of trade. For example, countries that speak the same language trade more with each other. Countries trade more with their former colonies and trade more with other countries that are the sources of a large number of immigrants. Countries that are part of preferential trade agreements have significantly higher volumes of trade than others.[7]

PART II

International Trade Policy

CHAPTER 4

Trade Policy Instruments: Tariffs, Quotas, Subsidies

As we have learned, international trade can affect domestic industries in different ways. Some domestic companies, faced with competition from lower-priced imports, will suffer losses, lay off workers, and go out of business. On the other hand, in response to higher world prices, some domestic companies will increase production to export, increase employment, and enjoy economic profits. Government policy makers will then be pressured to enact policies to protect their domestic firms and their workers from import competition and to promote their export industries. We start by examining policies designed to protect the import-competing industries.

Tariffs

A tariff is a tax that is imposed by a government on imports or exports. Virtually, every country in the world imposes tariffs on at least some imported products, and any multinational firm that imports finished or intermediate products is bound to encounter them.

An import tariff may be *specific*, expressed as a fixed amount of money per unit of the imported product. For example, a tariff of $100 may be placed on an imported bicycle. Tariffs may also be *ad valorem*, expressed as a percentage of the value of the product. For example, a 10 percent ad valorem rate may be placed on bicycles. If the value of the bicycle is $1,000, a tariff of $100 is collected by the customs agency. A *compound tariff* is a combination of both specific and ad valorem tariffs. For example, a $50.00 specific tariff per bicycle plus a 5 percent ad valorem tariff.

The value of the imported product can be calculated based on the price paid or payable for the product based on the Free (or Freight) on

Board (FOB) price or based on the Cost, Insurance, and Freight (CIF) price, which includes the cost of freight and insurance. All products shipped around the world are classified under the Harmonized Commodity Description and Coding system, commonly referred to as the "Harmonized System" (HS). The Harmonized System covers approximately 5,000 commodity groups, each identified by a six-digit code, arranged in a legal and logical structure. Well-defined rules support it to achieve uniform classifications around the world. More than 200 countries use the system as a basis for their customs tariff for the collection of international trade statistics and duty revenue.[1]

The Effects of a Tariff by a Small Country

The effects of a tariff depend on whether the imports of the country make up a small or large share of the world market. A small importing country is defined as one that has a small share of the total world supply of the product and will be unable to affect the world price. Suppose, in the absence of trade, the domestic price of a computer is $2,000 and 500,000 computers are supplied and demanded. Suppose the world price of computers is $1,000. Domestic consumers will then begin to buy the lower-priced computer imports, and the demand for domestic computers will decline, leading to a decrease in the price of domestic computers as well. Let us assume that the domestic consumers increase their quantity demanded by 100,000 to 600,000, while domestic producers decrease their quantity supplied by 100,000 to 400,000. This creates an excess demand for computers which is satisfied by the importation of 200,000 computers. Clearly, the domestic computer industry is adversely affected by competition from imports. Some of the companies leave the industry, and their workers will lose their jobs, which, in turn, hurts the communities where the companies were located. Inevitably, the industry will turn to the government for protection. In response to this pressure, the Home government places a specific tariff of $100 on computer imports.

---

[1]The United States' schedule is available at this site: https://www.usitc.gov/tata/hts/index.htm. (accessed September 23, 2017)

The tariff will increase the price of the computer by the full $100 to $1,100. Since the price of the imported computer has increased, domestic consumers will switch to domestic computers. The increase in the demand for domestic computers will, in turn, increase the price of domestic computers to $1,100. This increase in the price of domestic computers leads to an increase in the domestic quantity supplied of computers by say 50,000 units while decreasing the quantity demanded by say 40,000 computers. These effects will then reduce imports by 90,000 to 110,000.

Consumer Surplus, Producer Surplus, Deadweight Losses

To further analyze the effects of a tariff on the economy, we introduce the economic concepts of consumer and producer surplus. *Consumer surplus* is an economic measure of a gain to a consumer which is calculated as the difference between what a consumer is willing to pay for a product and the actual or market price that the consumer pays for the product. For example, assume a consumer goes out shopping for a personal computer and is willing to spend $1,500. If the price of the computer at the store is $1,000, then there is a gain in consumer surplus of $500. If the market price increases, then there will be a decrease in the quantity demanded and a loss in consumer surplus, and if the market price decreases, then there will be an increase in quantity demanded and a gain consumer surplus.

Producer surplus is an economic measure of a gain to a producer, which is calculated as the difference between the market price of the product which the producer receives after the sale of the product and the minimum price the producer is willing to accept for the product. Suppose a producer is willing to sell a computer for $1,500 and the market price is $2,000. If the producer sells the computer for $2,000, it will gain a producer surplus of $500. Producer surplus will increase if there is an increase in the market price and will decrease if there is a decrease in the market price.

So, an import tariff will result in a gain in producer surplus and a loss in consumer surplus. The government also gains, because the tariff generates more government revenue. Part of the total loss in consumer surplus is distributed to the producers as gains in producer surplus, and another part is distributed to the government as revenues. Two other parts of the loss are neither distributed to the government nor given to the producers. These losses are called the *deadweight losses* of the tariff. One part of the deadweight loss is called the *consumption loss*, which is due to the reduction in the total consumption of the computers. The consumers would have been willing to pay higher prices above $1,000 and up to $1,100 to get the additional 40,000 computers, yet the tariff prevents them from buying these computers. The second part of the deadweight loss is called the *production* loss or the *protective effect*. The tariff leads to an increase in domestic production by 50,000 units. The resources used to produce these additional units could have been used in producing other goods where the country has a comparative advantage. Thus, an import tariff leads to a net national loss.

The Effects of a Tariff by a Large Country

In some cases, a country's imports may be a large share of the world market, which means that any changes in the volume of imports by the country will affect the world price of the product. The effects of the tariff by a large country are similar to the small country case. The tariff raises the price of the product, increases domestic production, decreases domestic demand, and decreases the volume of imports. There will be a loss in consumer surplus, a gain in producer surplus, a gain in government revenues, and deadweight losses.

However, in the case of a large importing country, the decrease in the demand for imports will result in an excess supply of the product in the world market, which leads to a reduction in the world price. The reduction in the world price is a gain in the terms of trade of the importing country. Whether the country gains or loses with a tariff depends on the size of the terms of trade gain relative to the size of deadweight losses. If the deadweight losses are higher than the terms of trade gain, then the country loses. If the terms of trade gain is larger than the deadweight losses, then the country gains. Therefore, it is possible for a large country to improve its net national welfare by imposing a tariff. This gain to the country is a loss to the exporting country. This is an example of *beggar-thy-neighbor-policy*, where one nation gains at the expense of another nation. There is a possibility that the exporting country may retaliate and place a tariff on the exports of the importing country. In this case, when two large countries place tariffs on their own imports, both countries lose.

In addition to the net national welfare loss, a tariff can also adversely affect a country's exporters. If the tariff is levied on imported inputs, then the cost of imported inputs increases, which raises the overall costs of the exported product. Thus, higher costs lead to higher prices and reduced exports. This is why American car companies that import steel are opposed to a tariff on imported steel because it puts them at a competitive disadvantage in the world car market.

Furthermore, the decrease in imports leads to a decrease in the national income of the exporting country. This decrease in foreign country's national income results in decreases in the demand for imports. The reduction in the country's exports then leads to falling output and employment in the country's export industries.

Quotas

Another trade policy instrument designed to protect a domestic import-competing industry is a quota. An import *quota* is a restriction on the quantity of a product that can be imported, which is achieved by the government issuing quota licenses. An import quota license gives the holder the right to import a specific amount of the product during a specific time period.

The effects of a quota are very similar to the effects of a tariff. Given that a quota limits the supply of imports, it leads to an increase in the price of both the imported and domestic product. The rise in the price results in an increase in domestic quantity supplied and a decrease in domestic quantity demanded. Consequently, there will be a gain in producers surplus, a loss in consumers surplus, and the associated deadweight losses. The difference between a quota and a tariff is that with the quota, the government does not receive any revenues. With a quota, the difference between the world price of the good and the higher post-quota domestic price is called a *quota rent*. Quota rents are collected based on how the government allocates the licenses. Quota licenses can be allocated for free to domestic importing firms or individuals on a first-come-first-serve basis or on a proportional basis. In either way, the holder of the import licenses will pay the lower world price for the imports and then sell them at a higher price at home and collect the rents. Another way to auction the licenses is selling them on a competitive basis to the highest bidder. Here, the government collects the rents, similar to revenues collected through a tariff.

Another form of a quota is a Voluntary Export Restraint (VER). Under a VER, the exporting country agrees to limit its exports to the importing country. This usually happens after an importing country threatens to place tariffs or quotas on the exporting country's product. Faced with this threat, the exporting country can raise the price of its exports, thus capturing the quota rents.

Tariff Rate Quotas

Under the rules of the World Trade Organization (WTO), quotas on most manufactured products have been prohibited. WTO members have replaced quotas on agricultural products, textiles, and apparels with tariffs or *tariff rate quotas (TRQ)*. A TRQ allows a specified quantity of goods to be imported at a lower tariff rate (the *within quota rate*), whereas any imports above this level face a higher tariff rate (the *above quota rate*).

U.S. sugar imports are strictly controlled by TRQs. The volume of these quotas is established annually by the United States Department of Agriculture, and the United States Trade Representative (USTR) allocates the TRQs among countries. The North American Free Trade Agreement (NAFTA) has provided Mexico with tariff-free sugar exports into the American market since January 1, 2008. The Dominican Republic-Central American Free Trade Agreement (DR-CAFTA) also includes sugar provisions that provide those countries with guaranteed TRQs. Due to such quotas, American domestic raw sugar prices are 34 percent above world prices, leading to considerable losses in consumer surplus and gains in producer surplus. Foreign sugar exporters that had been allocated the right to sell sugar into the United States have also benefited from the rights.[2]

---

[2]C. Dewey. 2017. "Why Americans Pay More for Sugar," *The Washington Post*,. https://www.washingtonpost.com/news/wonk/wp/2017/06/08/why-americans-pay-more-for-sugar/?noredirect=on&utm_term=.73a3ef786314 (accessed August 9, 2017)

Other Barriers to Trade

Most governments rely on other instruments to erect barriers to trade. A *local content requirement* (*LCR*) is a regulation that requires that a minimum percentage of a product's total value must be produced domestically if the product is to qualify for zero tariff rates. The intended effect of these requirements is to pressure both domestic and foreign companies to use domestic workers or other inputs in the production of those products. LCRs are common in the automobile industry, particularly among developing countries, to shift their manufacturing base from assembly into the production of engines or transmissions. This regulation has similar effects as a quota, with the exception that it does not restrict the number of imports but allows the local companies to import and buy more domestic products.

Many countries have *government procurement laws* that require governments to purchase their goods and services from domestic producers. In the United States, for example, there are "Buy American" provisions for all levels of governments, particularly at the state and municipal levels. Government procurement laws allow domestic producers to charge a higher price than imports. In 1994, a select number of countries signed the WTO Agreement on Government Procurement, which granted each other equal access to government contracts, although certain government agencies were excluded from this agreement. Even though the United States signed the agreement, some bills passed by the U.S. Congress continued to have a "Buy American" requirement. To provide an economic stimulus to the economy during the Great Recession, the Congress passed the American Recovery and Reinvestment Act, which authorized about $275 billion to be spent on construction, maintenance, and repair of public buildings but required these projects to use domestic steel, iron, and manufactured products.

Governments commonly require goods to meet specific *technical regulations or standards* to be sold in the country. Such standards are designed to provide information about the product, ensure consumer safety, protect the environment, and guarantee product quality. Having too many standards can create problems for producers and exporters and can create a substantial barrier to trade. The WTO agreement includes the Technical

Barriers to Trade Agreement to make sure that regulations, standards, classification, and testing procedures do not create unnecessary barriers to trade. The agreement calls for countries to be nondiscriminatory in their use of regulations and to adopt international standards. Member countries are required to make public their rules and to notify the WTO of changes in their policies.[3] Governments also have *health and safety standards* for foods and medicines that can at times be used to restrict trade. Another WTO agreement, the Sanitary and Phytosanitary Agreement, establishes a basic set of rules for dealing with food safety and animal and plant health standards. Each country is permitted to set its own rules, provided these rules be based on science. A continuing dispute over health and safety standards is between the United States and the European Union over the use of growth hormones in American beef. In 1989, the European Union banned the imports of beef containing growth hormones. After several complaints by the United States, the WTO authorized the United States to impose retaliatory tariffs on EU agricultural exports. In 2009, both countries reached a temporary agreement that allows for increased access into European markets for American beef not treated with growth hormones and the elimination of American tariffs.[4]

Subsidies

Subsidies are used by governments to encourage exports or discourage imports. Direct subsidies are cash payments to producers, while indirect subsidies take a variety of forms, including price guarantees, low-interest loans, and tax breaks. An example of a direct subsidy is an *export subsidy*, which is a payment to firms for every unit exported, either a fixed amount or a fraction of the sales price.

The Effects of an Export Subsidy

Let Home be a shirt producer that can export shirts at a world price of $30. At this price, let the domestic quantity demanded be 100,000 shirts

---

[3]https://www.wto.org/english/tratop_e/tbt_e/tbt_e.htm.
[4]https://www.wto.org/english/tratop_e/dispu_e/cases_e/ds26_e.htm.

and the quantity supplied be 150,000 shirts, with the excess supply of 50,000 shirts to be exported. The government now provides a direct export subsidy of $10 per shirt. In response, suppose domestic shirt manufacturers increase the production of shirts by 30,000 shirts to 180,000. To receive the export subsidy, the producers reduce the supply of the shirts to the domestic market (since they do not receive the extra $10) and instead supply it to the world market. The decrease in the supply of the shirts in the domestic market leads to a rise in the domestic price and reduces the domestic quantity demanded by 20,000 to 80,000. Thus, export will increase by 50,000 to 100,000.

The increase in the domestic price leads to a loss in consumers surplus and a gain in producer surplus. The government has to pay the cost of the subsidy, which equals the level of exports multiplied by the $10 subsidy. There will also be a net national loss composed of a consumption effect and a production effect. The consumption effect is the loss in consumer surplus for those consumers who are unable to buy the product at the world price, and the production effect is the loss due to the artificial increase in domestic production. If Home is a major exporter in the world market, the increased supply of shirts exports will lead to a decrease in the world price of shirts, and it will experience a loss in its terms of trade.

WTO Rules on Subsidies

The WTO has a set of rules for subsidies that may promote exports. Direct subsidies to exports are prohibited, except export subsidies used by the lowest-income developing countries. Indirect subsidies that have an impact on exports are *actionable*, which means that the subsidy hurts the interests of other countries. If an importing country's government believes that a foreign country is using a prohibited or actionable subsidy that is injuring its domestic industry, it can either file a complaint with the WTO and use its dispute settlement procedure or impose a *countervailing duty*, a tariff to offset the price or cost advantage created by the subsidy to foreign exports.

WTO members agreed to abolish all export subsidies in agriculture by 2013, although this goal has not been achieved. Europe maintains a system of agricultural subsidies known as the Common Agricultural Policy

(CAP). The CAP began not as an export subsidy but as a price support program for European farmers. However, the price support is set at such a high level that it turned Europe from being an importer of food under free trade to an exporter. For example, the CAP pays sugar beet farmers a price that is five times the world price, which permits European farmers to sell the sugar at a much lower price than the world market price. As a result, Europe has become a significant exporter of sugar, even though countries in Central and South America have a comparative advantage in sugar production. A study estimated the welfare cost to European consumers exceeded the benefits to the farmers by nearly $30 billion.[5]

Strategic Trade Policy

In addition to the agricultural industry, the high-technology and manufacturing sectors of many countries receive subsidies. For example, both Europe and the United States provide subsidies to Airbus and Boeing, and the governments of Japan and South Korea have given direct subsidies to high-tech firms if they reach a certain level of export sales.

The use of subsidies to promote domestic companies is known as *strategic trade policy*. The theory behind this policy is that subsidies can help domestic companies capture economic profits from foreign competitors. These industries are essential to the country because they provide additional benefits known as positive externalities to other industries in the country.

An example of strategic trade policy is the aircraft industry, where Boeing and Airbus are the only producers of wide-bodied airplanes. Either company would have substantial profits if it were the only producer. Assume that either company produces the plane alone. It will capture the whole market and earn profits of say $100 million. However, if both companies produce the plane, then both will lose $5 million because their own sales revenues will be far less than the costs of manufacturing the planes. Which company will then produce and capture the profits? That depends on who produces first. Suppose Boeing has a head start and can

[5]P. Boulanger and P. Jomini. 2010. "Of the Benefits to the EU of Removing the Common Agricultural Policy," *Sciences Politique Policy Brief.*

produce the plane before Airbus. Airbus will then have no incentive to enter the market and Boeing will capture the whole market and earn $100 million.

Suppose the European government gives a $20-million research-and-development subsidy to Airbus to manufacture and enters the market. In this case, Airbus will earn a net profit of $15 million. Boeing will now realize that it will lose $5 million, so it will leave the market. The result is that Airbus will now earn $120 million.

The United States and the European Union have accused each other of using various subsidies to support their companies. European Union accuses the United States of subsidizing the research and development for the military versions of its planes, which is then used in the production of civilian planes. Also, both governments subsidize the interest rates that airlines pay when the companies borrow to finance the purchase of the planes.

In 1997 the United States and the European Union reached an agreement to limit their subsidies to the two companies. However, in 2004 the United States again claimed that the European Union provided Airbus with subsidies to launch a new super jumbo jet, the A-380, to directly compete with Boeing's existing 747. The European Union counterclaimed that the United States subsidized Boeing in the production of its new 787 Dreamliner and the 777X. In its latest ruling, the WTO decided that Airbus has received subsidies and the United States could retaliate by imposing tariffs.[6]

---

[6]https://www.wto.org/english/tratop_e/dispu_e/cases_e/ds316_e.htm.

CHAPTER 5

Arguments for Protection and the Political Economy of Trade Policy

We have demonstrated that even though a country gains from free trade, import-competing industries and their workers lose and seek protection from the government to erect barriers to trade, which ultimately results in a net national loss. If trade barriers are harmful to the nation, then why are they enacted? The erection of trade barriers depends on the mechanism through which trade policy is enacted. One method to have a direct vote is through a referendum. Let's suppose the domestic shoe industry is faced with competition from cheaper imports and asks the government to place a tariff on shoes. Assume there are five firms with a total gain in producer surplus of $500, and there are 10,000 consumers with a total loss in consumers surplus of $1,000. The government collects $300 in revenues, and the net national loss is $200. If there were a direct vote, since the number of consumers is greater than the number of firms and their workers, then the tariff would lose by a wide margin.

However, the act of voting is time-consuming and costly. The consumers would have to organize and inform the public about the adverse effects of the tariff on the consumers and the nation. In our example, the cost per consumer will be 10 cents. If the gain associated with voting to prevent the tariff is less than 10 cents, then the consumer will not bother to vote. There is also a *free-rider* problem. This problem happens whenever everyone in a group gains regardless of how much each group member contributes or does not contribute to preventing the tariff from being passed. So, a selfish individual will free-ride by letting others do the work of organizing the campaign to vote against the tariff. This free-rider problem becomes more serious when the number of individuals is large and widely dispersed. On the other hand, the five firms will find it in their interest to vote because the gain per firm will be $100, which outweighs the cost of campaigning and voting, and there is no free-rider problem.

In most countries, trade legislation is not passed by a direct vote through a referendum but is voted on by the elected representatives .Assuming that a politician's goal is to be elected or re-elected, the objective is to maximize the number of votes he or she receives in the next election. This is necessary if political rivalry exists, given that a politician who ignores the electorate will not be elected or driven out of office.

So, the different groups have an incentive to spend funds in an attempt to influence the election. Firms will make campaign contributions or hire lobbyists to persuade members of parliament or congress or the public of the need for tariffs and protection. Consumers, on the other hand, are unlikely to take an active role in the election or to finance a campaign for free trade because of the high cost of getting information about the impact of each policy. Also, the cost of raising funds from millions of consumers is much higher than the costs associated with raising funds from a small group of firms.

For example, the sugar quota system cost $4.4 billion to the U.S. consumers. It would be in the interest of American consumers to pressure the government to remove the quota. Yet, the annual loss amounts to only $11 per consumer or a little under $30 for a typical household. On the other hand, sugar processors and refiners have gained close to $4 billion, and they employ about 20,000 workers, so the producer gains from the quota represent an implied payment of about $200,000 per worker. It should be no surprise that these sugar producers are very effectively mobilized in defense of their protection. They have donated thousands of dollars to the campaigns of members of Congress and the American Sugar Alliance, the lobbying organization of the sugar industry, and spent millions of dollars to influence the vote on an agricultural bill that authorized the maintenance of the sugar quota system.

Arguments for Protection

There are many arguments for trade protectionism, which include terms of trade, revenue, domestic employment, cheap foreign labor, national security, infant industry, and to counter unfair trade practices.

The Terms of Trade Argument

As explained earlier, a tariff by a large country can lower the price of imports and thus produce a terms of trade gain. The terms of trade gain must be weighed relative to the deadweight losses of the tariff. The country's gain will be at the expense of the other country's loss, which may lead to retaliation by the other country.

The Domestic Employment Argument

The predominant argument for protection is the issue of jobs. Companies and their labor unions faced with import competition complain about the loss of jobs. On the other hand, as described earlier, tariff by an importing country decreases the foreign country's exports and national income. This causes the foreign country's national income to decrease which, in turn, reduces the foreign country's imports from the home country. This adversely affects the Home country's export industry and a loss of jobs.

Furthermore, a tariff on imported inputs raises the costs of production of finished products, placing the country's export industries at a global competitive disadvantage and leading to fewer exports and jobs. For example, in 2002, President George W. Bush put tariffs of up to 30 percent on imports of steel to protect domestic producers against low-cost imports. As a result, 200,000 Americans lost their jobs to higher steel prices and these lost jobs represented approximately $4 billion in lost wages. One out of four of these job losses happened in the metal manufacturing, machinery and equipment and transportation equipment, and parts sector. More American workers lost their jobs in 2002 to higher steel prices than the total number employed by the U.S. steel industry itself.[1]

The Cheap Foreign Labor Argument

American companies complain that they cannot compete with foreign low-wage countries, such as Mexico and China, and a tariff should be placed to equalize the difference in the wages. This argument fails to

---

[1] http://tradepartnership.com/reports/the-unintended-consequences-of-u-s-steel-import-tariffs-a-quantification-of-the-impact-during-2002-2003/.(accessed October 5, 2017)

understand the relation between wages, output per worker, and average costs. Suppose a Mexican worker's wage rate is five dollars per hour and an American worker's wage rate is twenty dollars per hour. The Mexican worker's productivity is 10 bicycles per hour, while the American worker's productivity is 50 bicycles per hour. The average cost of a bicycle in Mexico will be the cost per hour divided by output per worker or $0.50, while in the United States, it will be $0.4. Thus, even though the American worker gets paid four times more than the Mexican worker, the American worker is five times more productive than the Mexican worker, resulting in a lower average cost in the United States.

The United States is a capital and high-skilled labor-abundant country and has a comparative advantage in capital-intensive and high-skilled labor-intensive products. The workers in these industries are highly paid but also highly productive. On the other hand, the United States has a comparative disadvantage in low-skilled intensive products, which are less abundant in the United States. Industries that pay high wages not justified by high productivity will not be able to compete in the domestic or the world market.

Infant Industry Argument

This argument claims that a temporary tariff is necessary to protect the domestic infant industry against imports. The United States, based on the writings of Alexander Hamilton, the first secretary treasury, used this argument to place tariffs on its textiles, iron, and other industries against British competition. This argument is also used by developing countries to encourage their manufacturing industries. These countries do not have the same production technology and cost advantages as the established industries in the developed countries.

By placing a tariff or a quota, the government can limit foreign access to the domestic market, thus permitting the domestic industry to expand. After several years of protection, the domestic firms will find ways to lower their costs and effectively compete with the foreign firms both domestically and globally. The validity of this argument depends on whether the benefits exceed the costs. The gains in producer surplus to the industry and the country will happen in the future, while the deadweight losses occur in the present. This argument is valid if the present value of future gains is higher than the current national losses.

Although this argument is plausible, it must be qualified in several respects. First, once a tariff is placed, it is difficult to remove it, even after the protected industry has achieved cost efficiencies. Second, it is difficult to determine which industry has the potential to grow and achieve a comparative advantage in the future. Third, there are alternative government policies, such as a domestic production subsidy, which does not affect domestic prices and hence domestic consumption.

The Unfair Trade Practices Argument

This argument intends to protect a domestic industry from foreign competition due to unfair trade practices. We have already described one primary unfair trade practice is the use of production subsidies to promote exports. The WTO members are permitted to impose countervailing duties to offset the cost or price advantage created by the subsidizing country.

Another trade practice is *dumping*, which is selling a product at a lower price in the export market than at home. There are three different types of dumping. Sporadic dumping is temporary and designed to sell the excess supply of a product by lowering the price in the export market. Predatory dumping is to eliminate the domestic competition and capture the foreign market. The foreign company becomes the single producer that can then raise the price. This strategy is successful if the expected future profits are high enough to compensate for the losses incurred by selling the product at the lower price. Furthermore, the existence of high profits may encourage the domestic companies to enter the market. Persistent dumping is a form of price discrimination that is practiced by companies that have market power. A company can charge a different price for the same product if it can determine its customers' willingness to pay. It will then charge a higher price to consumers who are willing to pay a higher price and a lower price to consumers less willing to pay the price. When a company has market power at home but faces competition in the world market, it can charge a higher price at home and a lower price abroad.

In many countries, including the United States, a domestic company can appeal to the government and ask for protection. This usually takes the form of an antidumping tariff set as the difference between the home price and the export price. The WTO rules allow countries to retaliate against dumping if the dumping causes serious injury to the import-competing firms.

The National Security Argument

Some industries, such as the weapons industry, the steel industry, and some strategic technology industries, are vital to the national security of a country. In peaceful times, imports may capture a significant share of the markets for these products and reduce the size of these industries. However, in the case of a war, imports may be stopped, and the country will not have an adequate supply of these products for national defense. To protect against this possibility, these industries argue that they must be protected. In the United States, Congress passed the Trade Expansion Law of 1962, which allows the president to levy tariffs if "an article is being imported into the United States in such quantities or under such circumstances as to threaten or impair the national security."[2] This is a misguided argument because the government can stockpile the necessary inputs, such as steel, aluminum, or oil, by buying large quantities during peacetime, when they are less expensive and store them. Also, in the event of a war with an adversary, the government can acquire the materials from its allies. Another problem with this argument is to determine which industries are essential to national defense. Many industries produce inputs for other industries, for example, lumber for wood products, aluminum and steel for finished metal products, cotton for textiles, and others. Why should only one or two of these sectors get protection from imports?

The Cultural Identity Argument

This argument is to protect the cultural industries of a country, which include movies, television programs, music, newspapers, theater, and art. Countries complain that the global dominance of the United States in

---

[2]https://www.commerce.gov/news/fact-sheets/2017/04/fact-sheet-section-232-investigations-effect-imports-national-security.

the entertainment industry and pop culture will lead to a reduction in their domestic industries and threaten the cultural identity of the country. For example, in Europe, at least half of TV broadcasting time must be allocated to European films, television programs, and video-on-demand services to promote European artistic works.[3]

Public Revenue Argument

For many developing countries, where it is difficult to collect income and property taxes, tariffs can be collected at a lower cost at ports and border crossings. In the United States, before the imposition of the personal income taxes, import tariffs were a significant source of government revenues.

---

[3]https://ec.europa.eu/digital-single-market/en/promotion-and-distribution-european-works.

CHAPTER 6

The World Trade Organization, International Trade Relations and Issues

On June 17, 1930, the U.S. Congress passed the United States Tariff Act of 1930, also called the Hawley-Smoot Tariff Act, which raised import tariffs by 20 percent to protect American firms and farmers, adding substantial pressure to the international economic environment of the Great Depression. It was the last U.S. congressional policy which set actual tariff rates. The Act raised the United States' already-high tariff rates, which were enacted in 1922 to protect American farmers from declining prices due to European overproduction.

In response to the stock market crash of 1929, protectionist feelings grew in Congress and the president of the United States, Herbert Hoover, consequently signed the bill. Within 2 years, over 20 foreign countries adopted similar tariffs, making worse an already-depressed world economy and reducing global trade. American trade with Europe fell by some two-thirds between 1929 and 1932, while overall global trade declined by similar levels in the 4 years that the legislation was in effect.

In 1934, President Roosevelt signed the Reciprocal Trade Agreement Act, reducing tariff levels and promoting trade liberalization and cooperation with foreign governments. From 1934 to 1947, the United States entered into more than 30 bilateral tariff agreements, and over this period, the average level of tariffs fell to about half of the 1934 levels.

In 1947, the United States and some of its allies began trade negotiations under a new set of rules that became known as the General Agreement on Tariffs and Trade (GATT). Under the terms of the agreement, countries began to meet periodically, called Rounds, to reduce tariffs and settle trade policy issues. The first five rounds were organized around reducing tariffs on specific products. With the Kennedy Round (1964–1967), countries negotiated an across-the-board percentage reductions in tariffs for a range of goods. The Tokyo Round (1973–1979) established rules on subsidies and prohibited export subsidies on manufactured goods but not agricultural goods or textiles and apparel. The Uruguay Round of GATT, which started in 1986, addressed these issues, and after over 7 years of negotiations completed the round and led to the creation of the World Trade Organization, which began operations in 1995, and today has grown to 164 countries.

The ninth major round of trade negotiations began in 2001 in the city of Doha, Qatar. Known as the Doha Development Round, its aims were to decrease farms subsidies by developed countries; reduce tariffs on manufactured goods by the developing countries; reduce tariffs on textiles and apparel that poor countries cared about; free up trade in services; and negotiate rules in four new areas—competition, investment, government procurement, and trade facilitation. After years of negotiations, the developing countries refused to accept the large reduction in their industrial tariffs in exchange for greater access to the agricultural markets of the rich countries, ending the negotiations in 2008.

Some of the key provisions of GATT (WTO) are as follows:

1. Member countries cannot discriminate against each other. Every member must extend *most favored nation status* (MFN) to all other members. This means that if a country lowers tariffs on one trading partner, then those lower tariffs must be given to every other WTO member.
2. A country is permitted to temporarily raise tariffs when the imports cause or threaten serious injury to domestic producers. These are called safeguard and escape clause provisions.
3. Countries are permitted to form free trade areas and customs unions if the tariffs with the outside parties are not higher or more restrictive than the tariffs before the formation of the agreements.
4. Foreign goods should receive national treatment; that is, they should be treated similarly to the same ways that domestic goods are treated once they enter a nation's markets.[1]

[1]https://www.wto.org/english/thewto_e/thewto_e.htm (accessed October 25, 2017)

The WTO has several essential functions. It ensures that the member countries implement the reductions in tariffs and other trade barriers. It periodically conducts a trade policy review of its members to make sure that members comply with its rules and agreements. WTO also has a "dispute settlement" process, which formalizes the process by which member countries can settle their trade disputes. Under this process, if a country accuses another country of violating the WTO rules, it can bring the case to the WTO. WTO will then select a panel of experts to hear the case and reach a conclusion. The guilty party can appeal the decision, and the case can be brought before an appellate body to review the case. If the appellate body agrees with the lower body, then the guilty country must correct its policy to abide by the WTO rules. If the country refuses to comply, then the WTO grants the country that filed the complaint the authority to retaliate.

The General Agreement on Trade in Services

The Uruguay Round also created the General Agreement on Trade in Services (GATS), which covers most rules for trade in services. Member obligations under GATS are similar to the ones under trade in goods: that is, MFN treatment, market access, and national treatment. The GATS covers all services except the services provided by the government and air transportation services.

According to GATS, there are four modes of supplying services: cross-border trade, consumption abroad, commercial presence, and presence of natural persons. Cross-border supply is defined to cover services flows from one country to another country, such as banking services transmitted via telecommunications or mail. Consumption abroad refers to situations where a person travels to another country as a tourist or a patient. Commercial presence implies that a country provided a service in another country by establishing a physical presence, such as a hotel chain. Presence of natural persons consists of persons of one country entering another member country to supply a service such as accounting, teaching, or medical services subject to residency rules set by the host country.[2]

---

[2]https://www.wto.org/english/tratop_e/serv_e/gatsqa_e.htm. (November 24, 2017)

The Agreement on Trade-Related Aspects of Intellectual Property Rights (TRIPS)

A large volume of the value of international trade is in the form of trade in intellectual property, knowledge, and branding. The Uruguay Round introduced intellectual property rules into the multilateral trading system for the first time, and members of GATT signed the Agreement on Trade-Related Aspects of Intellectual Property Rights (TRIPS).[3] Prior to TRIPS, other agreements had been established to protect intellectual property, such as the Paris Convention for the Protection of Industrial Property, the Berne Convention for the Protection of Literary and Artistic Works, and the World Intellectual Property Organization (WIPO).

The main instruments used to protect intellectual property are copyrights, trademarks, patents, industrial design, trade secrets, and test data. An interesting instrument is *geographical indication*, which is a name or an indication associated with a place that is sometimes used to identify a product. This geographical design does not only say where the product comes from but, more importantly, it identifies the product's unique characteristics, which are the result of the product's origins. Well-known examples include Champagne, Scotch Whiskey, Tequila, Darjeeling, and Roquefort cheese. Sparkling wine can only be named Champagne only if the grapes are grown in the Champagne region of France, and Tequila can only be produced in Mexico.

Intellectual property protection of pharmaceutical products has become a significant issue between the developed and developing countries. Developing countries complain that these patent protections make these drugs extremely expensive, which creates a public health problem in their countries. Drug companies argue that without patents, new drugs would not be developed due to their high costs of development and production. Another problem is with counterfeit products. Many brand name goods are sold in other countries with counterfeit trademarks, leading to loss of sales of the original brands and loss of reputation due to the poor quality of the counterfeit products.

---

[3]https://www.wto.org/english/thewto_e/whatis_e/tif_e/agrm7_e.htm.

Developing countries see technology transfer as part of the bargain in which they have agreed to protect intellectual property rights. The TRIPS Agreement aims for the transfer of technology and requires developed country members to provide incentives for their companies to promote the transfer of technology to least-developed countries to help them create a solid technological base.

International Trade and Labor and Environmental Issues

In recent years, the United States and other advanced countries have demanded that labor and environmental standards be included in trade negotiations. Labor standards refer to all issues that directly affect workers, such as health and safety standards, the use of child labor, minimum wages, and the right to form unions. Consumer groups are concerned about the poor working conditions and "sweatshops" in poor developing countries. Labor unions are concerned that the absence of minimum wages and lack of collective bargaining in those countries gave an unfair cost advantage to those countries, thus threatening jobs in the advanced economies. In response to these demands, corporations have started to monitor and improve the working conditions of their overseas plants and contractors. However, in practice, this monitoring is inadequate and has led to major industrial tragedies, such as the collapse of a garment factory in Bangladesh in 2013, which killed more than a thousand workers. Shortly after the disaster, Walmart and other American and European retailers stopped buying garments from certain factories based on the suppliers' poor record of safety standards. Some governments have relied on the use of trade barriers to enforce labor standards. The U.S. administration under President Obama dropped Bangladesh from the list of countries eligible for a program called the Generalized System of Preferences, which gives low tariff to low-income countries.

Some proponents of trade barriers sometimes use the issue of labor standards as a means of protecting the domestic industries and their workers. This explains why many developing countries are opposed to labor standard negotiations by the developed countries. There is a suspicion that efforts by developed countries for labor standards are a way to weaken the comparative advantage of low-income countries in such industries as textiles and apparel, which require an abundance of low-skilled, low-productivity, and low-wage workers.

Another concern of proponents of trade barriers is that developing countries intentionally lower their labor standards to attract foreign direct investment. In practice, there is little or no evidence that countries use low labor standards to invite foreign investment. While there is evidence that a country can reduce production by prohibiting the formation of labor unions, there is no evidence that this type of policy has given any country a comparative advantage that it did not already have. Many of these low-income countries have not only low labor standards but also poor roads, ports, power supply, schools, and telecommunications, which discourages foreign investment.

Many opponents of free trade claim that trade is harmful to the environment and thus propose putting trade barriers to enforce environmental standards. It is true that industrial production can lead to environmental damage, but we must distinguish between environmental impacts that remain within the country and those that cross national boundaries.

Opponents of trade barriers to enforcing environmental standards claim that compliance with domestic environmental standards increases the cost of production and will reduce the competitiveness of firms. This encourages countries to lower their environmental standards to stay competitive. Furthermore, it causes countries with high environmental standards to move their production facilities to countries with low standards. This was an argument against North American Trade Agreement (NAFTA), where opponents of the agreement claimed that American companies would move their operations to Mexico, which had lower environmental standards, in addition to lower labor standards.

The other concern with environmental problems is when one country's pollution spills over to another country and when the combined industrial production of many countries leads to global problems like the depletion of the ozone layer and climate change. The WTO does not deal directly with the environment but allows countries to adopt their laws concerning environmental issues, provided these laws do not discriminate against foreign companies operating in the country. Instead, global environmental issues are addressed through international agreements such as the Kyoto Protocol, which successfully eliminated the use of chlorofluorocarbon, which contributed to the depletion of the ozone layer. In 2015 more than 190 nations met in Paris and agreed on a plan to limit climate change by submitting national plans to reduce carbon emissions, with the United States withdrawing from the accord in 2017.

Preferential Trading Arrangements

An alternative to multilateral negotiations to trade liberalization is the formation of preferential trading arrangements (PTA) among two or more countries. There are several types of PTAs.

A *free trade area* (FTA) is when two or more countries agree to remove all tariff and nontariff barriers among themselves. Each member nation is permitted to set its own set of trade restrictions against nonmembers. An example is NAFTA between the United States, Canada, and Mexico which has been renegotiated and re-named, the United States Mexico Canada Agreement (USMCA) The United States also has FTAs with Australia, Chile, Israel, Columbia, and a host of other countries.

A *customs union* is an agreement between two or countries to remove all tariffs and nontariff barriers between themselves. Also, a customs union establishes a common external tariff and other trade restrictions against nonmembers.

The fact that an FTA does not have a common external tariff as does a customs union leads to a problem with FTAs. For example, suppose the United States has a higher tariff on Chinese bicycles than Mexico or Canada. China can export the bicycles to either Canada or Mexico and then ship them to the United States. To prevent this action, FTAs have *rules of origin* that specify what type of goods can be shipped duty-free within an FTA. For example, under NAFTA rules at least 60 percent of the product must be produced within the three countries to qualify for duty-free status.

A *common market* is a customs union that also allows for the free movement of factors of production across national borders within the economic bloc. The European Union is an example of a common market.

Effects of Preferential Trading Arrangement

Suppose in the United States the price of a shirt is $20.00, while in Canada, it is $8.00 and in Mexico, it is $6.00. Under these circumstances, the United States will import shirts from Mexico, since Mexico is the lowest-cost producer. Now suppose the United States sets a 100 percent ad valorem tariff on all shirts made in Mexico and Canada. The price of shirts in Canada increases to $16.00, and the price of the Mexican shirt rises to $12.00. In this case, the United States continues to import all its shirts from Mexico.

Suppose the United States establishes a free trade agreement with Canada and removes the tariff on Canadian shirts while keeping the tariff on Mexican shirts. In this case, the price of Canadian shirts falls from $16.00 to $8.00, with the Mexican shirts price remaining at $12.00. The United States will now import all shirts from Canada since it is cheaper than Mexican shirts.

The formation of this FTA has two effects on the volume of trade. First, there is a shift away from the lowest-cost Mexican producer to the lowest-cost FTA producer. This shift is called *trade diversion*, which reduces world welfare because the United States no longer imports from the country that has a comparative advantage. Resources are directed away from shirt production in the low-cost world producer, Mexico, and directed toward shirt production in the higher-cost partner, Canada. The second effect is the expansion of trade between the United States and Canada is called *trade creation* which increases the welfare of the two countries.

Whether the formation of the FTA is beneficial to the United States and Canada depends on the relative strengths of the forces of trade diversion and trade creation. Let's examine the welfare effects of the formation of the FTA in the United States. Consumers will benefit because the price of the shirts falls from $12.00 (the Mexican price plus the tariff) to $8.00. Producer surplus falls due to the fall in the price of the shirt. The government loses the tariff revenues because it no longer imports from Mexico and Canadian imports are tariff-free. The gain offsets part of this loss in government revenues to the consumers in the form of lower prices. The remainder is a net loss to the United States because the American consumers now pay a higher price for the Canadian imports than the Mexican imports. The difference in the price between the Canadian shirt and Mexican shirt times the quantity of shirt imported diverted from Mexico to Canada represents the cost to the United States of trade diversion.

Because trade expands between the United States and Canada, however, there are gains. The drop in the price of shirts results in real production and consumption effects. Overall, the United States is better off if the benefits of trade creation with Canada are greater than the losses of trade diversion from Mexico.

WTO members are obliged to notify the WTO when they form a PTA. PTAs are discriminatory since countries in a PTA deny MFN status to non-PTA members. WTO has allowed PTAs under the assumption that the trade creation exceeds the trade diversion. The latest PTA is the Trans-Pacific Trade Partnership (TPP), which establishes an FTA among 12 countries that border the Pacific Ocean: Australia, Brunei, Canada, Chile, Japan, Malaysia, Mexico, New Zealand, Peru, Singapore, Vietnam, and the United States. In 2017, President Trump decided to leave the partnership agreement.

PART III

International Finance

CHAPTER 7

An Introduction to Open Economy Macroeconomics and the Balance of Payments

The economy of a nation is composed of four sectors: household, business, government, and foreign. The household sector supplies resources or factors of production, such as land, natural resources, capital goods, and labor, to the business sector. The business sector pays for these factors of production through the sale of the goods and services. The government collects taxes from the households and businesses and spends the tax revenues on goods and services. The foreign sector includes spending by the rest of the world on a nation's exports, which is a source of income, which is then spent by households and firms on imports.

Gross domestic product (GDP) is a measure of the value of all final goods and services produced in the domestic economy. GDP can be measured by adding all the expenditures on this output by the four sectors of the economy. *Personal consumption expenditures, C,* are goods and services bought by households. *Gross private domestic investment, I,* is spending by businesses on machines, tools, and equipment, and on building homes and factories. *Government purchases, G,* are the spending by the government sector on goods and services, and wages and salaries of government employees. *Net exports goods and services, NX,* are equal to exports minus imports.

GDP can also be measured by summing all the incomes generated through the production of the goods and services. These incomes include wages and salaries, interest income, rent, and other incomes generated through the production of goods and services. So, the value of a nation's output is identical to its national income.

The Balance of Payments

The *balance of payments* is a record of all the transactions between the residents of a country and the rest of the world during a given time period. The primary purpose of the balance of payments is to inform the government of the international economic and financial position of the country and to help it in the formulation of economic policies.

The balance of payments accounts are maintained according to the accounting rules of double-entry bookkeeping. Every international transaction has both a credit and a debit side. Any transaction that leads to a payment by a foreigner to a resident of the country is a *credit* and is recorded as a positive sign, while any transaction that leads to a payment by a resident of a country to a foreign resident is a *debit* and is recorded as a negative sign.

From an American perspective, the following transactions that lead to the receipt of dollars from the rest of the world are entered as credits: goods and services exports, income received from investments abroad, gifts received from foreign residents, aid received from foreign governments, and foreign direct and portfolio investments in the United States.

Conversely, the following transactions that lead to a payment of dollars to the residents of the rest of the world are recorded as a debit: imports of goods and services, income paid to foreigners on their investments in the United States, gifts to foreign residents, aid given to foreign governments, and American direct and portfolio investments in other countries.

The balance of payments has three separate accounts: the current account, the capital account, and the financial account.

Current Account

The current account measures the value of exports and imports of goods and services plus net income earned on portfolio investments plus net unilateral transfers.

The *merchandise trade balance* includes the values of exports and imports of goods. In addition to merchandise trade, a country also exports and imports services. Examples of services trade are tourism, transportation, education, insurance, banking, legal services, and technical services.

For example, the money spent by American tourists on vacation abroad is considered imports of foreign tourist services, while the money spent by foreign tourists in the United States is considered U.S. tourism exports. Adding the services trade balance to the merchandise trade balance gives us the *goods and services balance.*

The current account also measures the income received by Americans from foreign investments, such as stock dividends, bond interest payments, and income paid by foreign employers to Americans working abroad, minus the income paid to foreigners on their investments in the United States and income paid to foreign employees working in the United States.

The final item in the current account is *net unilateral transfers.* These transfers include private and government aid to foreign countries in cases of natural disasters or conflicts minus donations from foreign individuals and organizations to American charities.

Capital Account

The capital account consists of capital transfers and the purchase and sale of certain nonfinancial transactions. An example of a capital transfer is when a government forgives a foreign loan. Other examples include companies' sale and purchase of rights to natural resources, patents, copyrights, trademarks, franchises, and leases.

Financial Account

The financial account measures international financial flows through the purchase and sale of financial assets. These include portfolio investments, such as the purchase and sale of corporate stocks and bonds; government bonds; as well as changes in bank claims and liabilities. Bank claims include loans, overseas deposits, and other short-term instruments; claims on affiliated banks abroad; and foreign government obligations. Bank liabilities include demand deposits, savings deposits, certificates of deposits, and liabilities of affiliated banks abroad.

From a bookkeeping perspective, any transaction that results in a *financial inflow* is recorded as a credit. A financial inflow occurs under the following cases: (1) whenever foreigners buy American stocks and bonds, (2) when an American bank receives a loan repayment by a foreign company, (3) when a foreign company builds a factory in the United States, and (4) when an American company sells one of its factories in another country to a resident or a domestic company of the country. Similarly, a *financial outflow* is recorded as a debit and implies the opposite of these transactions.

The financial account also includes changes in the country's central bank holdings of *international reserve assets*, which include foreign currencies, short-term foreign government securities, assets issued by the International Monetary Fund known as Special Drawing Rights, and gold.

Theoretically, the sum of the balance of payments entries must equal to zero. If the United States has a current account deficit, it must finance it by borrowing or selling some of its assets, which translates into a financial account surplus. Because some data on international transactions are inaccurate or unavailable, the last item called *statistical discrepancy* is created to make sure the balance sums to zero.[1]

The Current Account and the Macroeconomy

The current account can also be related to a nation's domestic production, income, and expenditures. As described earlier,

$$GDP = C + I + G + NX$$

Net exports are the largest component of a country's current account (CA), so we can express

$$GDP = C + I + G + CA$$

Another measure of a country's GDP is by adding all the incomes that are generated by the process of producing all the goods and services,

---

[1] See https://apps.bea.gov/iTable/iTable.cfm?ReqID=62&step=1.(accessed January 6, 2018)

which is referred to as national income (Y). A country's national income is saved, spent, or paid in taxes. So

$$Y = C + S + T$$

where S is equal to private saving and T represents taxes. Since the value of production must equal the value of income, we can set the two equations equal as follows:

$$GDP = Y$$

$$C + I + G + CA = C + S + T$$

Subtracting C from both sides, we get:

$$I + G + CA = S + T$$

Rearranging the terms gives us:

$$I + CA = S + (T - G)$$

The term $(T - G)$ represents the budget of the government or public saving. Next, we add S (private saving) to $(T - G)$ to arrive at national savings, denoted as S^*. So,

$$I + CA = S^*, \text{ and rearranging}$$

$$S^* - I = CA$$

Thus, if a country saves more than it invests, it will have a current account surplus and will be a net lender, which shows as a financial accounts deficit. Conversely, if a country invests more than it saves, it will have a current account deficit and will be net borrower which shows as a financial account surplus. Current account deficits must be financed by borrowing from abroad through the sale of domestic assets to the rest of the world, and current accounts surpluses lead to lending to the rest of the world through the purchase of foreign assets. If the total domestic assets owned by the rest of the world is subtracted from the total foreign assets owned by the country, we arrive at the country's *net international investment position*.[2] The United States has had large current account deficits since the early 1980s and a negative net investment position, making it the world's largest debtor nation.

---

[2]Ibid.

CHAPTER 8

The Foreign Exchange Market

The foreign exchange market is a global market where currencies and financial instruments denominated in different currencies are traded. According to the Bank for International Settlements, in 2016, the total value of daily foreign exchange transactions averaged about $5.1 trillion dollars. The dollar accounted for 88 percent of all these transactions followed by the euro, the yen, and the pound. A third of these transactions are carried out in London, followed by New York, Singapore, Hong Kong, and Tokyo.[1] The major participants in the foreign exchange market are individuals, corporations, investors, speculators, commercial and investment banks, foreign exchange dealers and brokers, and central banks. A very small percentage of the trading in the foreign market involves the physical exchange of one currency for another currency. Most transactions are electronic transfers of balances between commercial banks and foreign exchange brokers and dealers.

Commercial banks are the most important participants in the foreign exchange market. Banks enter this market on behalf of their corporate customers. For example, suppose Apple corporation wants to pay £2 million to a British parts supplier. First, Apple contacts its American bank, say Citibank, and requests a quotation for selling dollars and buying pounds. If the rate is acceptable, for example, $2.00 per pound, it instructs Citibank to deduct $4 million from its checking account and pay £2 million to the supplier's British bank, say Barclays. Citibank

---

[1]Bank for International Settlements. December 11, 2016. *Triennial Central Bank Survey of Foreign Exchange and Derivatives Market Activity in 2016.* https://www.bis.org/publ/rpfx16.htm. (accessed February 24, 2018)

instructs its correspondent bank in London, say, Lloyds, to transfer pounds from its checking account to the British company's checking account at Barclays.

Banks also enter this market to trade currencies from each other. These foreign currency transactions take place in the wholesale market, where about 20 major banks trade with one another in the *interbank market*. The top largest foreign exchange dealers by market share are Citi, J.P. Morgan, UBS, Bank of America Merrill Lynch, Deutsche Bank, HSBC, Barclays, Goldman Sachs, Standard Chartered, and BNP Paribas.[2]

Foreign exchange dealers buy and sell currencies from their accounts, whereas foreign exchange brokers, unlike dealers, do not buy and sell currencies, but they match buyers and sellers and receive a fee for their services.

Foreign exchange traders can obtain information about exchange rates from major commercial information distributors, such as Thompson Reuters and Bloomberg. Traders can then contact each other to obtain actual rates and negotiate deals. When a trade is agreed upon, banks communicate and transfer funds through SWIFT (Society for Worldwide Interbank Financial Telecommunications), a communications network, which electronically connects more than 11,000 banks and broker/dealer in more than 200 countries and processes more than 15 million transactions a day. After the confirmation of the deal, the trade in dollars is settled, and funds are transferred either through the Clearing House Interbank Payments System (CHIPS) or in euros through the Trans-European Automated Real-time Gross Settlement Express Transfer (TARGET).

Foreign Exchange Instruments

Spot contracts: In the spot market, currencies are traded for immediate delivery, which is about 2 days after the transaction has been concluded.

Forward contracts: Forward contracts are created to buy or sell currency for future delivery at a rate called the *forward rate*, which is set today in the forward market.

---

[2]See https://www.euromoney.com/article/b18f5s6kqtcr6m/euromoney-fx-survey-2018-results-released. (accessed February 24, 2018)

Futures contracts: A futures contract is a promise that the two parties holding the contract will deliver currencies to each other at some future date at a predetermined exchange rate. Futures contracts are standardized, mature at certain regular dates, and can be traded on an organized futures exchange like the International Money Market of the Chicago Mercantile Exchange.

Swaps: A foreign exchange swap combines a spot sale of a foreign currency with a forward repurchase of the same currency. These contracts are used by corporations to reduce the transactions costs of foreign exchange trading.

Options: A foreign currency option contract provides an option holder the right to buy or sell a fixed amount of a currency at a prearranged price within a specified time. A *call option* gives the holder of the option the right, not the obligation, to buy foreign currency at a specified period, and a *put option* gives the right to sell foreign currency at a specified price. The price at which the option can be exercised is called the *strike price*.

The Exchange Rate

An exchange rate is the price of a currency relative to another currency or the rate at which one currency can be traded for another currency. There are two ways to quote a currency pair, either directly or indirectly. A *direct currency quote* is simply a currency pair in which the domestic currency is the quoted currency, while an *indirect quote* is a currency pair where the domestic currency is the base currency. So, if you were looking at the Mexican peso as the domestic currency and U.S. dollar as the foreign currency, a direct quote would be USD/MXN, while an indirect quote would be MXN/USD. The direct quote varies the domestic currency, and the base, or foreign currency, remains fixed at one unit. In the indirect quote, on the other hand, the foreign currency is variable, and the domestic currency is fixed at one unit. For example, if Mexico is the domestic currency, a direct quote would be 17.75 USD/MXN, which means that one U.S. dollar will purchase 17.75 pesos. The indirect quote for this would be the inverse (1/17.75), 0.056 MXN/USD, which means with 1 peso, you can purchase US$0.056. In the foreign exchange spot market, most currencies are traded against the U.S. dollar, and the U.S. dollar is frequently the base currency in the currency pair.

However, not all currencies have the U.S. dollar as the base. The British pound, Australian dollar, New Zealand dollar, and the euro are all quoted as the base currency against the U.S. dollar. In these cases, the U.S. dollar is the counter currency, and the exchange rate is referred to as an indirect quote. Therefore, the EUR/USD quote is given as 1.20, for example, meaning that the price of 1 euro is 1.20 dollars.

Like all prices, exchange rates also change over time. If the exchange rate of the euro rises from $1.25 to $1.30, it is called an *appreciation* of the euro. If the exchange rate of the euro falls from $1.25 to $1.20, it is called a *depreciation* of the euro. We can also measure the rate of appreciation or depreciation of a currency. In our example, when the rate of appreciation of the euro is equal to 4 percent which is calculated as the difference between the two rates divided by the initial rate multiplied by a hundred.

Exchange rate changes are important because they will affect the price of a country's exports and imports. Suppose a pound of French cheese costs 10 euros and the exchange rate is $1.25. Then the price of the cheese in dollars will be equal to $12.50. If the euro depreciates to $1.20, then the price of the cheese in dollars decreases to $12. Similarly, suppose the price of an American computer is $1,000 and the exchange rate is $1.25. Then the price of the computer in euros will be equal to 800 euros. At a rate of $1.20, the price of the American computer increases to 833.33 euros. Therefore, a euro depreciation makes French exports cheaper and imports more expensive. The depreciation leads to an increase in French exports and a decrease in French imports of American computers.

The Real Exchange Rate

The exchange rate described so far is referred to as the nominal exchange rate. There is another definition of the exchange rate, namely, the *real exchange rate*. The nominal exchange rate is how much of a foreign currency that you can purchase with a unit of the domestic currency. The real exchange rate measures the rate at which two countries' goods trade with each other. . . . Let P_{US} be the U.S. price level, and P_{FRENCH} be the

French price level. The real exchange rate will then be equal to the nominal exchange rate multiplied by the ratio of the two price levels.

The real exchange rate can change if there are changes in the two countries' price levels or changes in the nominal exchange rate. To determine the impact of exchange rate changes on a country's net exports, we must consider changes in the country's real exchange rate rather than only the changes in the nominal exchange rate.

Recall that when the euro depreciated in nominal terms, the dollar price of the French cheese declined. Now suppose the price of cheese increases to 10.41 euros. With an exchange rate of $1.20, the dollar price of the cheese remains unchanged at $12.50. Even though the nominal exchange rate depreciated, the real exchange rate remained constant. Now, suppose, the price of the American computer declines to $960. Then with an exchange rate of $1.20, the euro price of the computer remains at 800 euros. Again, we can see that while the nominal rate depreciated, the real rate remained the same.

The Effective Exchange Rate Index

Over time a currency may appreciate relative to one currency and depreciate relative to another currency. To determine whether a currency has appreciated or depreciated relative to a selected set of currencies, we can construct *an effective exchange rate index*. To build the index for a currency, we first select a basket of currencies of the country's major trading and financial partners. Next, we select weighs for each currency within the basket, reflecting the importance of the trading partner. Finally, we select a base year, which serves as a reference point in time. The value of the index in the base year is equal to 100. For example, if 2012 were the base year, the value of the index in 2012 would be 100. If the value of the index were 120 in 2016, then the index has increased by 20 percent. Many effective exchange rate indices are available from both private and public sources, including the United States Federal Reserve System, the European Central Bank, the International Monetary Fund, the Bank for International Settlements, the Bloomberg Spot Dollar Index, the J.P. Morgan index, and the *Wall Street Journal*. Similar to the real exchange rate, we can also construct a real effective exchange rate index, which includes changes in the price levels of the countries in the basket.

CHAPTER 9

The Determination of the Exchange Rate

Let us look at the exchange rate of the British pound relative to the dollar. Based on the law of demand, as the price of pounds increases, the quantity demanded decreases, and as the price decreases, the quantity demanded rises. Suppose the exchange rate is £1 = $1 and a British sweater costs £100. Then the British sweater will cost $100, and Americans demand a certain quantity of sweaters. Now suppose the pound depreciates to £1 = $0.50. Then the price of the British sweater declines to $50. This reduction in the price of the British sweaters leads to an increase in the quantity demanded of sweaters by Americans and an increase in the quantity demanded of pounds.

The quantity supplied of pounds is positively related to its price; the higher the price of the pound, the higher the quantity supplied. Again, suppose the exchange rate is £1 = $1, and an American pair of shoes costs $200. Then the shoes will cost £200, and the British will demand a certain quantity of shoes. If the pound appreciates to £1 = $2, then the price of the American pair of shoes declines to £100, which leads to an increase in the quantity demanded of shoes by the British. The appreciation leads to an increase in the quantity supplied of pounds to purchase dollars to purchase the shoes.

The equilibrium exchange rate is when the quantity supplied is equal to the quantity demanded. If the actual exchange rate is above the equilibrium exchange rate, we have a surplus of pounds, which leads to a depreciation. If the actual exchange rate is below the equilibrium exchange rate, then we have a shortage of pounds, which leads to an appreciation of the pound.

Changes in the supply and demand for pounds will lead to changes in the equilibrium exchange rate. An increase in the demand for pounds leads to a shortage of pounds and a pound appreciation, while a decrease in the demand for pounds leads to a surplus of pounds and a pound depreciation. An increase in the supply of pounds leads to a surplus of pounds and a pound depreciation, while a decrease in the supply of pounds leads to a shortage and a pound appreciation. Let us examine the determinants of changes in the supply and demand for a currency in the short run and the long run.

Determination of Exchange Rates in the Long Run

Four factors change exchange rates in the long run: relative national price levels, relative national income levels, changes in consumer tastes and preferences, and trade barriers.

Relative Price Levels

If the British price level rises relative to U.S. price level, Americans will decrease their demand for the relatively more expensive British goods, leading to a decrease in the demand for British goods and a decrease in the demand for pounds. On the other hand, the British will increase their demand for the relatively cheaper American goods, leading to an increase in the supply of pounds. The decrease in the demand and the increase in the supply of pounds will lead to a surplus of pounds and a depreciation of the pound. Therefore, an increase in the price level of a country relative to another country will lead to a depreciation of the currency in the long run.

Relative Growth Rates

Growth in the British economy means rising incomes and increased spending by the British citizens on American imports, and an increase in the demand for dollars (hence an increase in the supply of pounds) leading to l a depreciation of the pound. Growth in the U.S. economy means rising incomes and increasing imports from Britain, an increase in the demand for pounds, leading to an appreciation of the pound.

Consumer Tastes and Preferences

An increase in British tastes and preferences for American goods and services leads to an increase in the supply of pounds and a pound depreciation. Alternatively, an increase in American tastes and preferences for British goods and services leads to an increase in the demand for pounds and a pound appreciation.

Trade Barriers

American barriers to trade on British imports lead to a decrease in the demand for pounds and a pound depreciation, while British import barriers on American goods lead to a decrease in the supply of pounds and a pound appreciation.

Determination of Exchange Rates in the Short Run

The most important cause of changes in the exchange rates in the short run is international financial capital flows. Over 90 percent of all activity in the foreign exchange market is in investment in assets denominated in different currencies. Investors compare the expected rate of return on domestic assets with the expected rate of return of foreign assets in deciding whether to invest in a domestic or foreign asset.

Suppose an American investor is deciding whether to invest in an American Treasury bond or in a British Treasury bond (called a gilt) for 1 year. Let the annual interest rate on the American bond equal 5 percent and the British bond equal 6 percent. The expected rate of return on the American bond is equal to the American interest rate of 5 percent. Let us now look at how to calculate the expected rate of return of the British bond. To purchase a British bond, we must first purchase pounds at today's spot rate. Then we invest in the British bond and after 1 year earn 6 percent. After 1 year, we convert the pound earnings into dollars at the existing spot rate in a year from now. However, we do not know the future spot rate, so we have to make an expectation about the future spot rater. Suppose today's spot rate is $2.00 and we expect the spot rate in 1 year to be $2.02, which is equivalent to an expected rate of appreciation of

1 percent. Then the total expected return on the British bond will equal the interest rate on the British bond interest plus the expected appreciation of the pound. In our example, the expected return on the British bond equals 7 percent. We observe that the British bond has a higher expected return than the American bond.

If a British bond has a higher expected return than an American bond, then American investors will find British bonds more attractive and will increase their demand for pounds to invest in the British bond. On the other hand, British investors will find American bonds less attractive and reduce their purchases of American bonds, which will lead to a decrease in their supply of pounds. The increase in the demand for pounds combined with the decrease in the supply of pounds leads to a shortage of pounds in the foreign exchange market and a pound appreciation.

Furthermore, the increase in the demand for British bonds will lead to an increase in the price of those bonds and a decrease in the British interest rate, and the decrease in the demand for American bonds will lead to a decrease in the price of American bonds and an increase in the American interest rate.

Now suppose we expect the spot rate in a 1 year to be $1.96, which is equivalent to a 2 percent depreciation of the pound. The expected return on the British bond will then equal 4 percent. Since the British bond has a lower expected return, American investors will find British bonds less attractive and will decrease their purchases of the bond and hence decrease their demand for pounds. On the other hand, British investors will find American bonds more attractive and will increase their supply of pounds to purchase the bonds. The decrease in the demand for pounds, combined with the increase in the supply of pounds, leads to a surplus of pounds in the foreign exchange market and a pound depreciation.

Similarly, the decrease in the demand for British bonds will lead to a decrease in the price of the bonds, and an increase in the British interest rate and the increase in the demand for American bonds will lead to an increase in the price of American bonds and a decrease in the American interest rate. These changes in the spot rate and interest rates due to international capital flows will lead to the equality of the expected return of both assets. This equality of expected returns is called the *interest parity condition*, which states:

| Expected return on a domestic asset | = | Interest rate on a foreign asset + Expected appreciation of the foreign currency (or the expected depreciation of the domestic currency) |

Given the interest rates on the domestic and foreign assets and the expected change in the exchange rate, there is a single spot rate, called the equilibrium exchange rate, that equates the two expected returns.

The equilibrium spot exchange rate will change in the short run if there are changes in the two interest rates and the expected future spot rate. Holding the other variables constant, if the interest rate on British assets rises, then British assets will have a higher expected return and become more attractive, leading to an appreciation of the pound. Similarly, if the interest rate on American assets rises, then American assets become more attractive, leading to a depreciation of the pound. Finally, if expected future spot rate rises, then British assets will have a higher expected return, leading to a pound appreciation.

The Market for Money and the Determination of Interest Rates

Functions of Money

There are four functions of money: medium of exchange, unit of account, store of value, and standard of deferred payment. The first function of money is a medium of exchange or a means of payment. Thus, the dollar is the medium of exchange in the United States, the pound in Britain, the peso in Mexico, and other currencies in their respective countries.

The second function of money is a unit of account, which is a way of measuring the value or the price of a good or service. We use meters to measure distance and kilograms to measure weight. We use dollars to measure the value of goods in the United States. Money can function as a store of value or wealth. Wealth is the accumulations of savings which occurs when a household's income exceeds expenditures.

Wealth is held in many different forms, including money. The last function of money is a standard of deferred payment, where money can be used to pay off debts.

The Market for Money and Interest Rates

The quantity or the supply of money in the economy equals the sum of the total amount of currency in circulation plus the value of all the checking account at banks. The central bank of a country determines the supply of money in the country by directly controlling the amount of currency in circulation and indirectly controlling the amount of checking accounts that banks can create. Changes in the supply of money are at the discretion of the central bank.

Households and firms demand money—that is they plan to hold money—to pay for their purchases of goods and services. From a macroeconomic perspective, the ability of households and firms to spend on goods and services depends on the country's national income. If the economy expands and national income rises, then spending increases, leading to an increase in the demand for money. Conversely, if the economy contracts and national income falls, then spending decreases, leading to a decrease in the demand for money.

Wealth can be held in the form of money or other assets. Whether an individual holds money or other assets depends on their expected returns. The return on money as an asset is zero, whereas other assets have a positive expected return. By holding money, we give up the opportunity of earning a return on an interest-bearing asset. Thus, the higher the interest rate, the higher the opportunity cost of holding money, and therefore, the lower the demand for money.

The supply of money is set by the central bank and is independent of the interest rate, whereas the demand for money is inversely related to the interest rate. The interest rate that equates the supply and the demand for money is called the equilibrium interest rate. If the actual interest rate is above the equilibrium interest rate, there will be a surplus of money and a decline in the interest rate. Conversely, if the actual interest rate is below the equilibrium interest rate, there will be a shortage of money and a rise in interest rate. The equilibrium interest rate will change if there are changes in the supply and demand for money.

Suppose the central bank increases the supply of money. This creates an excess supply of money, which means that individuals now hold more money than they desire. They will then reduce the excess money balances by lending it to others. This increase in lending will result in a decrease in the interest rate. If the central bank decreases the money supply individuals now hold less money than they desire. They will then borrow to satisfy their increased demand for money, which leads to an increase in the interest rate.

Interest rates can also change if there are changes in the demand for money. An increase in national income during an economic expansion leads to an increase in spending and the demand for money. With no change in the supply of money, there is a shortage of money and an increase in the interest rate. Conversely, a decrease in national income leads to a decrease in the demand for money and a decrease in interest rates.

Money Supply, the Interest Rate, and the Exchange Rate in the Short Run

Suppose the central bank of the United States, known as the Federal Reserve Bank, lowers the American interest rate by increasing the domestic money supply. As described earlier, the decrease in the American interest rate will lead to a lower expected return on American assets, making them less attractive to British investors. The lower expected return on American assets leads to a decrease in the British demand for American assets and hence a decrease in the demand for dollars. On the other hand, American investors will find British assets more desirable and will increase their demand for British assets and hence will increase their supply of dollars to purchase the British assets. The decrease in the demand and the increase in the supply of dollars create a surplus of dollars in the foreign exchange market and a dollar depreciation. Thus, an increase in a country's money supply causes its currency to depreciate, and a decrease in a country's money supply causes its currency to appreciate.

Money, the Price Level, and Exchange Rates in the Long Run

We now examine how changes in the money supply affect exchange rates in the long run. The *law of one price* states that an identical product has the same price wherever the product is sold. For example, suppose the price of a pair of shoes is $400 in Boston, and the identical pair of shoes is $500 in New York. Then a person can buy the shoes in Boston and sell them in New York and make a profit of $100. This action will increase the demand for shoes and increase the price of shoes in Boston and increase the supply of shoes and decrease the price in New York until the price of the shoes is equal in both cities.

To compare the price of the shoes in two different countries, we need to know the price of shoes in each country and the exchange rate to convert the price of the product in each respective country. If the two prices are not equal, people will buy the shoes in the lower-priced country and sell them in the higher priced country. These actions will then result in changes in the exchange rate until both prices become equal.

To test the law of price, the magazine *The Economist* invented the Big Mac Index to measure the equilibrium value of a currency. A Big Mac is a hamburger that is sold by McDonald's in over a hundred countries across the globe. The index suggests that a Big Mac should cost the same wherever it is sold given the existing exchange rates. If it did not, then the exchange rate would change to make the prices equal. For example, suppose a Big Mac costs $5.00 in New York, and it costs 150 rupees in New Delhi. If the exchange rate were 50 rupees per dollar, then the dollar price of the Big Mac in New Delhi would be $3, which is $2 (or 44.4 percent) cheaper than in New York. Based on the law of one price, the exchange rate that would equate the price of the Big Mac in both locations should be 30 rupees per dollar (150 rupees divided by $5). Thus, the rupee was 40 percent undervalued. In theory, we could buy Big Macs in New Delhi for $3 and sell them in New York for $5. The purchase of Big Macs in New Delhi would increase the price of Big Macs there, and the sale of Big Macs in New York would decrease the price there. The purchase of Big Macs in India would increase the demand for rupees, leading to an appreciation of the rupee until it reaches its equilibrium rate. The law of price does not happen for several reasons. The law of price applies to only products that are tradable across countries, and it ignores transportation and other costs of production. Although *The Economist* considered the index as a fun way to test the law of one price, it has proven to be a relatively useful predictor of exchange rate changes. https://www.economist.com/news/2018/07/11/the-big-mac-index.

We can extend the law of one price for a single identical product to a basket of goods to arrive at the purchasing power parity (PPP) theorem, which states that the exchange rate between two countries equals the ratio of the countries' price levels. For example, if a basket of goods in the United States costs $200 and £100 in Britain, then according to the PPP theorem, the exchange rate should be £1 = $2. If the cost of the basket of goods in the United States rises by 10 percent to $210, then at the exchange rate of $2 per pound, British goods become less expensive. Americans will increase their demand for British goods, and the British will decrease their demand for American goods. The change in prices leads to an increase in the demand for pounds and a decrease in the supply of pounds, which leads to an appreciation of the pound and a depreciation of the dollar. Thus, an increase in a country's price level relative to another country's price level leads to a depreciation of the currency.

Another form of the purchasing power parity, known as *relative purchasing power parity*, examines the rate of change in the price levels and exchange rates over time. The relative purchasing power parity states that the rate of depreciation of a currency depends on the country's inflation rate relative to another country's inflation rate. For example, if the British inflation rate is 5 percent and the U.S inflation rate is 3 percent, the pound will depreciate by 2 percent over time.

Money, Price Levels, and Inflation

The relative purchasing power parity states that in the long run, changes in exchange rates depend on changes in the inflation rates between two countries. A country's inflation rate depends on changes in the rate of growth in the money supply relative to the rate of growth in the economy.

The *quantity theory of money* explains the link between the supply of money and the price level. Recall that people demand money as a medium of exchange, which depends on national income. The quantity theory of money is based on the *Equation of Exchange* stated as:

$$M = k \times P \times Y$$

where M is the supply of money, P is the price level, and Y is the level of real national output. The expression $P \times Y$ represents national income, and *k* indicates the proportion of national income that is held as money. So, the expression ($k \times P \times Y$) is the national demand for money. In the long run, *k* is relatively constant, and *Y* depends on the supply of a country's resources, such as labor, natural resources, capital, and technology. Based on the equation of exchange, we can arrive at the quantity theory of money, which states that in the long run, the supply of money will be equal to the demand for money ($k \times P \times Y$). According to the quantity theory, given a constant *k* and *Y*, if a central bank increases the supply of money, it will only lead to an increase in the price level in the long run. Converting the quantity equation into rates of change we get:

> the rate of growth in the money supply = rate of change of *k* + rate of change of the price level (inflation rate) + rate of growth of *Y*.

With *k* constant, we can rearrange the equation and get:

> the rate of inflation = the rate of growth in money supply − the rate of growth in real output

For example, if the United States' economy is growing at 2 percent in the long run, and if the Federal Reserve Bank allows the money supply to grow by 5 percent, then the United States will have a 3 percent inflation rate. Similarly, if the British economy is growing at 3 percent, and if the Bank of England allows the money supply to increase by 8 percent, then the British will have a 5 percent inflation rate. Based on the relative purchasing power parity, then the rate of change of a currency will depend on the difference between the inflation rates of the two countries. In our example, the British inflation rate is 3 percent higher than the American inflation rate and the pound is expected to depreciate by 3 percent in the long run.

Exchange Rate Overshooting

Changes in the expected future exchange rate can lead to *exchange rate overshooting*, where the exchange rate changes by a larger percentage in the short run than in the long run. Suppose the Bank of England increases the rate of growth of the money supply by 8 percent. Holding everything else constant, then according to relative purchasing power parity theorem, investors will expect the pound to depreciate by 8 percent in the long run. However, in the short run, many prices are slow to adjust and will remain rigid, so we will not experience an immediate 8 percent inflation rate. In the short run, the increase in the money supply leads to a decrease in the British interest rate. The combination of lower British interest rates and the decrease in the expected future spot rate lowers the expected return on British assets by more than 8 percent. Over time, as prices begin to rise, and British interest rates begin to rise, the pound will appreciate to its long-run value of 8 percent. Therefore, in the short run, the pound overshoots its long-run equilibrium exchange rate.

The Effects of Exchange Rate Changes on the Current Account

Changes in a country's exchange rate affect a country's exports and imports. Suppose the price of a British computer is £1,000. If the exchange rate is $2.00 per pound, the dollar price of the computer will equal $2,000. Now suppose the pound falls to $1.98, a 10 percent depreciation of the pound. The price of the computer in pounds will remain at £1,000, but the dollar price of the computer will fall to $1,980.00 This reduction in the price of the computers will lead to an increase in British computer exports.

Similarly, let the price of an American motorcycle be $5,000. At an exchange rate of $2.00, the pound price of the motorcycle will be £2,500. Again, let the pound depreciate by 10 percent to $1.98. Then, the dollar price of the motorcycle will remain at $5,000, but the pound price of the motorcycle will increase to $2,525.25. This increase in the price of the motorcycle would lead to a decrease in motorcycle imports. Therefore, depreciation of a currency should increase the country's net exports and improve its trade balance. The extent to which the trade balance is affected depends on several factors.

The Elasticity of Demand for Exports and Imports

The price elasticity of demand is defined as the responsiveness of buyers to changes in the price of a product. The price elasticity of a product is equal to the percentage change in the quantity demanded divided by the percentage change in the price. Suppose there is 10 percent fall in the price of a product and buyers respond by increasing their purchases by 20 percent. Since the percentage change in the quantity demanded is greater than the percentage change in the price, the demand for the product is price elastic. If the buyers respond by increasing their purchases by less than 10 percent, then the demand for the product is price inelastic.

A nation's balance of trade is equal to the value of its exports minus the value of its imports. Whether a country's trade balance improves following a deprecation depends on the foreign elasticity of demand for the nation's exports and the domestic elasticity of demand for the nation's imports. The general rule is that the trade balance will improve if the sum of the nation's elasticity of imports, plus the foreign demand elasticity for the nation's exports, is greater than one. The trade balance will worsen if the sum of the elasticities is less than one, and the trade balance will not change if the sum is equal to one.

Let us look at an example of whether a depreciation will improve or worsen the trade balance. The percentage change in the value of exports is equal to the percentage change in the volume of exports plus the percentage change in the price of the product, while the percentage change in the value of the imports is equal to the percentage change in the volume of imports times the percentage change in the price of the product. Assume the British demand elasticity for imports equals 0.6, and the American demand elasticity for British exports equals 0.8. The sum of the two elasticities equals 1.4. A 10 percent depreciation of the pound will increase the pound price of the American motorcycle by 10 percent, and given the import price elasticity of 0.6, the quantity demanded of imports will decrease by 6 percent. Thus, the net effect on the pound value of imports is a reduction of 4 percent.

On the other hand, the 10 percent depreciation of the pound will decrease the dollar price of the British computers by 10 percent. Given the American export elasticity of demand of 0.8, the 10 percent depreciation will increase exports by 8 percent. Given no change in the pound price of the computer, the total value of exports in pounds increases by 8 percent.

Therefore, with the sum of the elasticities greater than one, the depreciation led to 6 percent reduction in the value of imports and an 8 percent rise in the value exports, resulting in a 4 percent improvement in the trade balance.

Let us now look at the case where a depreciation worsens the trade balance. Suppose the British elasticity for imports is 0.3 and the American demand elasticity for British exports is 0.2; the sum of the elasticities is 0.5. The 10 percent depreciation of the pound raises the pound price of British imports by 10 percent and a 3 percent reduction in the quantity demanded of imports. The depreciation leads to a 7 percent increase in the value of imports. The pound price of British exports is unaffected by the 10 percent depreciation, whereas the dollar price of exports decreases by 10 percent. British exports to the United States increase by 2 percent, resulting in a 2 percent increase in the value of British export. Thus, the British trade balance worsens by 1 percent.

The J-Curve Effect

If the demand for imports both at home and abroad is inelastic, it is possible for the trade balance to worsen immediately following a depreciation and improve over time. However, over time the elasticities begin to rise, and the current account begins to improve. The changes in the current account following a depreciation resemble the letter *J*.

The quantity and price in a trade contract are set in advance. For example, the British importer of American motorcycles is likely to enter a contract with the American company to import a specific quantity at some future period. The terms of the contract will also fix the price of the motorcycle. Such a contract provides guarantees to the American exporter that the motorcycles will be sold and provides guarantees to the British importer that the price of the motorcycles will remain fixed. Most contracts are for a year or more.

The consequence of short-term contracts of less than a year is that both the local prices and quantities of imports and exports are fixed for the length of the contract. A depreciation of the pound results in an immediate increase in the value of imports and a decrease in the value of exports measured in pounds, which worsens the trade deficit.

Following the depreciation, when contracts begin to be renegotiated, traders will change the quantities demanded. Since the pound depreciation causes the American motorcycles to become more expensive to British residents, the quantity of imported motorcycle demanded and purchased will fall. Similarly, British computers will become cheaper to

Americans, so as their contracts are renegotiated, they will begin to increase their demand for British computers. Thus, as time passes, the effects from the changes in quantities will exceed the price effect caused by the pound depreciation, and the trade balance will improve.

Exchange Rate Pass-Through

The *J*-curve analysis assumes that a depreciation of the exchange rate will result in a proportionate increase in the price of imports. In practice, there may be a less-than-proportionate change, diminishing the effect of the increase in the price on the volume of imports. The extent to which a change in the exchange rate leads to a change in the price of the import and export prices is called *exchange rate pass-through*.

Assume that the price of British computer exports to the United States is fixed at £1,000.00. At an exchange rate of $2.00 per pound, the dollar price of the computer is equal to $2,000.00. Let the pound appreciate by 10 percent, from $2.00 to $2.20. If the British firm does not change the pound price of the computer, the dollar price of the computer will increase by 10 percent to $2,200.00. Thus, there is a complete pass-through of the 10 percent depreciation of the pound into a 10 percent increase in the price of the computer.

The full 10 percent increase in the price of the computer could lead to a substantial decrease in sales in the United States. If the American market is a significant share of the British company's global sales, the company can choose not to pass on the full change in the price due to the pound appreciation by lowering the pound price of the computer. For example, the British company may lower the pound price of the computer by 5 percent from £1,000.00 to £950.00, so that the dollar price of the computer rises from $2,000.00 to $2,090.00 or a 4.5 percent increase in price, resulting in an incomplete pass-through.

Exchange Rate Risks and Multinational Corporations

Multinational corporations face the risk of foreign exchange fluctuations. The degree to which a company is affected by foreign exchange rate changes is called foreign exchange exposure. There are three types of foreign exchange exposure: translation exposure, transaction exposure, and operating exposure. *Translation exposure*, also called accounting exposure, comes from the need to convert the financial statements of a company's foreign operations from the foreign currency to the home currency. If the exchange rate changes from one period to another period, the value of the company's assets, liabilities, revenues, costs, profits, and losses that are denominated in the foreign currency will result in foreign exchange losses or gains. *Operating exposure* measures the change in the company's future revenues and costs due to a change in the exchange rate. Finally, transaction exposure measures the change in the value of a country's contracts that are entered at present but are settled in a later date. To manage the transaction exposure, a company can use the forward market.

The Forward Market

Suppose a British computer manufacturer orders some chips from Intel, an American company. The chips will be delivered in 3 months and will cost $10 million. At the time of the order, the spot exchange rate is $2.00. The British company then budgets £5 million to be paid when it receives the chips. The British firm faces the risk of a pound depreciation. If in 3 months the spot rate depreciates to $1.95, then the cost of the order will equal £5.1282, an increase of £128,200.

A company can cover or *hedge* this risk by contacting a bank to arrange for a forward contract. The company signs an agreement today with the bank to buy $10 million at a 90-day forward rate of $1.98. In 3 months, the company pays £5.050505 to the bank and receives $10 million to pay Intel.

Now suppose a British exporter has shipped computers to an American company and expects to be paid $10 million in 3 months. During this period, the exporter faces a risk of a pound appreciation. At today's $2.00, the company expects to receive £5.0 million. If the pound appreciates to $2.04, then the company will receive only £4.9 or £100,000 fewer pounds. To hedge against the risk, the company can contract with a bank to sell $10 million at a rate of $2.01 and receive £4.975 million.

The forward market allows importers and exporters to transfer the risk of foreign exchange fluctuations to commercial banks. Commercial banks can minimize the foreign exchange risk by matching forward purchases from exporters with forward sales from importers.

At any given date, the forward rate may be equal to or different from the spot rate. If the forward rate is higher than the spot rate, then the currency is said to be at a *forward premium*, and if the forward rate is less than the spot rate, then the currency is said to be at a *forward discount*.

Forward Exchange Rates and Covered Interest Parity

A currency's forward exchange rate is determined by the currency's spot rate and the interest rates on assets denominated in the two currencies. Once again, suppose an American investor is deciding whether to invest in a U.S. Treasury bond or a British Treasury bond for 1 year. Let the annual interest rate on the American bond equal 5 percent and the British bond equal 6 percent, and let today's spot rate be equal to $2.00. The British bond has a higher interest rate, but by investing in the British bond, the investor faces a risk of a pound depreciation. To avoid the exchange rate risk, the investor can enter a forward contract to sell the principal and interest on the British bond based on today's forward exchange rate. The return on the British bond would then equal:

British bond interest rate + (forward rate − spot rate)/spot rate.

If this return is greater than the American bond return, which is equal to the American interest rate, then the American would invest in the British bonds. The buying of spot pounds will increase the spot rate, and the selling of forward pounds will decrease the forward rate. The movement of funds from the United States to Britain increases the American interest rate and decreases the British interest rate. These changes continue until the expected returns on both assets become equal. This equality of returns is called the *covered interest parity condition*, which states:

American bond return (interest rate) = British bond interest rate + (forward rate − spot rate)/spot rate

Rearranging,

American bond interest rate − British bond interest rate =
(forward rate − spot rate)/spot rate

The expression (forward rate − spot rate)/spot rate is called the *forward premium* on pounds (or *forward discount* on dollars). Based on the covered interest parity condition, if the American interest rate is greater than the British interest rate, then the pound must be at a forward premium, and if the American interest rate is less than the British interest rate, then the pound is at a forward discount.

PART IV

Macroeconomic Policies in an Open Economy

CHAPTER 10

Aggregate Demand, Aggregate Supply, Output, and Exchange Rates

Aggregate Demand

Another way to explain the identity of total expenditures and total output in an economy is in terms of the aggregate demand and aggregate supply in the economy. *Aggregate demand* is the quantity of the goods and services (GDP) demanded by the households, firms, the government, and the rest of the world at different price levels. The price level is defined as the average prices of goods and services in the economy at a point in time. One such measure in the United States is called the *consumer price index* (CPI), which is a weighted average of the prices paid by consumers for a typical basket of goods and services. The *producer price index* is the weighted average prices that businesses pay for inputs. Finally, the GDP deflator is an index of the average prices for all goods and services in the economy, including consumer goods, investment goods, and exports. The quantity of aggregate demanded is inversely related to the price level. There are several reasons for this negative relationship.

First, households usually hold some of their wealth in the form of money, savings accounts, stocks, bonds, and other forms of financial wealth. A lower price level increases the purchasing power of this wealth. This increase in household wealth leads to more spending on products and services. Second, the price level affects the households' demand for money. A lower price level means that households do not need to hold as much money as before and may transfer some of the excess money into savings accounts at banks. Banks could then use the funds to make loans to businesses. Competition among banks will lower the interest rates, which then encourages businesses to borrow funds to invest in plant and equipment. Third, when the price level falls, domestic goods become cheaper relative to foreign goods, leading to an increase in exports and a decrease in imports.

In addition to changes in the price level, household spending can change if there are changes in household wealth, the level of household debt, consumer confidence, interest rates, and income taxes.

For example, in the United States, the housing market crash and the stock market decline in 2008 and 2009 resulted in decreases in household wealth, which led to decreases in household spending and aggregate demand. Similarly, a loss in consumer confidence can lead to a decrease in aggregate demand. High household debt restricts access to future borrowing, which reduces household spending on cars and appliances. High interest rates can also lead to lower spending on durable goods, as the cost of borrowing to finance those purchases increases. An increase in personal income taxes decreases households' disposable income which also leads to lower household spending.

Consumer sentiments about the economy can also affect spending. If households feel more confident about their financial and employment security, they will then increase their spending, and if household confidence declines, then spending will decline.

Business investment is affected by changes in interest rates, business confidence, taxes, and business regulations. Lower interest rates reduce the cost of borrowing, leading to higher investment spending. Business optimism about the future increases investment, while business pessimism decreases investment. Lower business taxes and fewer regulations increase business investment.

Net exports are affected by changes in the exchange rate, domestic national income, foreign national income, and barriers to trade. If the currency depreciates, then exports become cheaper and imports more expensive, leading to an increase in net exports. Higher domestic national income leads to more imports, while higher foreign national income leads to higher exports. Tariffs and other barriers to trade lead to lower imports and higher net exports.

Aggregate demand can also change as a result in changes in monetary and fiscal policies.

Aggregate Supply

Aggregate supply is the total quantity of output produced at different price levels. The goal of every firm is to maximize profits. Profits are equal to total revenues, which is equal to price times the quantity sold, minus the total costs of production. If the costs of production remain constant, but the price increases, then firms find it profitable to increase production and sales. Therefore, the quantity of aggregate supply is positively related to the price level.

In addition to changes in the price level, aggregate supply can change if there are changes in the price of inputs, new technologies, taxes, and business regulations. An increase in the prices of factors of production, such as wages or energy costs, increases the costs of production and decreases aggregate supply. New technologies that improve productivity and lower costs lead to an increase in aggregate supply. Higher taxes and more business regulations raise business costs and decrease aggregate supply.

Macroeconomic Equilibrium

At a certain price level, called the equilibrium price level, aggregate demand equals aggregate supply. If the actual price level is higher than the equilibrium price level, then aggregate supply will be higher than the aggregate demand and a surplus of goods and services in the economy. The surplus puts pressure on the price level to decline, which increases the quantity of aggregate demand and decreases the quantity of aggregate supply. If the price level is below the equilibrium level, then aggregate demand will be higher than aggregate supply and shortage. In response to this shortage, firms will increase price and/or increase production.

Equilibrium GDP and the price level can change with changes in aggregate demand and aggregate supply. An increase in aggregate demand with no change in aggregate supply leads to a shortage, which then leads to an increase in the price level and GDP. A continuous increase in aggregate demand results in a continuous increase in the price level, which is called inflation. A decrease in aggregate demand with no change in aggregate supply leads to a surplus, which, in turn, leads to a decrease in GDP, which is called a recession, and a reduction in the price level.

A continuous decrease in aggregate demand results in a continuous decrease in the price level, which is called deflation.

An increase in aggregate supply with no change in aggregate demand leads to a surplus, which leads to an increase in GDP and a decrease in the price level. Conversely, a decrease in aggregate supply leads to a reduction in GDP and an increase in the price level.

Fiscal Policy and Aggregate Demand

Fiscal policy refers to the changes in government spending and taxation to achieve a set of economic goals. If the government wants to increase national output and income and decrease unemployment, it engages in an expansionary fiscal policy. This policy involves a combination of increases in government spending and/or decreases in taxes. An increase in government spending directly increases aggregate demand, while a decrease in income taxes increases households' after-tax income, which increases consumer spending. Expansionary fiscal policies result in a government budget deficit, which adds to the national debt. If the government decides to reduce deficits and the national debt, it pursues a contractionary fiscal policy, which includes a combination of decreases in spending and increases in taxes, which will reduce aggregate demand.

Fiscal Policy, Interest Rates, and Exchange Rates

Suppose the British government faced with a stagnant economy and rising unemployment decides to use an expansionary fiscal policy to increase aggregate demand. This expansionary fiscal policy leads to a government budget deficit, which must be financed by borrowing. The increased demand for borrowed funds in the credit market increases the British interest rate. If the British interest rate rises above the American interest rate, then as explained earlier, British assets become more attractive to Americans, increasing the demand for pounds in the foreign market. At the same time, British investors will decrease their demand for American assets, which reduces the supply of pounds. The increase in the demand and decrease in the supply of pounds leads to a pound appreciation. The appreciation of the pound will then negatively affect British net exports and decrease aggregate demand. The reduction in net exports partially offsets the expansionary effect of the initial fiscal policy.

Monetary Policy and Aggregate Demand

Every nation has a central bank. Sweden was the first country to establish a central bank in 1668 followed by the creation of the Bank of England in 1694. In 1913, the U.S. Congress created the central bank known as the Federal Reserve System. In 1999, the central banks of eleven European countries —Austria, Belgium, Finland, France, Germany, Ireland, Italy, Luxembourg, the Netherlands, Portugal, and Spain—formed the *European System of Central Banks*, established the European Central Bank, and created the euro. In 2001, Greece adopted the euro, followed by Slovakia, Slovenia, Lithuania, Latvia, Malta, Cyprus, and Estonia.

The primary function of a central bank is to conduct monetary policy. Most central banks have the responsibility to maintain stable prices by adopting a target for inflation. The Federal Reserve is also responsible for maintaining high employment. The main channel by which monetary policy affects economic activity is by changing interest rates. When the central bank decides to change interest rates, it relies on its monetary policy instruments to change the level of funds, called *reserves*, that banks have available for lending. Central banks have several monetary policy instruments to control the level of bank reserves. The most frequently used instrument is called *open market operations*. Open market operations refer to the purchase and sale of government-issued securities in the open market for these securities by the central bank.

When the central bank buys government securities from banks and the public, it pays for them by increasing bank reserves. Banks are then able to use the reserves to give loans to businesses. These loans increase the supply of money, which results in a reduction in interest rates. The lower interest rate encourages firms to borrow from banks and increase their investment, leading to an increase in aggregate demand and GDP.

When the central bank sells government securities to the banks or the public, it lowers bank reserves. Lower reserves lead to a decrease in loans and a reduction in the supply of money. The reduction in the money supply leads to an increase in interest rates. The increase in interest rates leads to a decrease in business investment, which, in turn, leads to a decrease in aggregate demand and real GDP.

Monetary Policy, Interest Rates, and Exchange Rates

Suppose the Bank of England wants to increase aggregate demand by increasing the money supply and lowering British interest rates. If the British interests decrease relative to American interest rates, then, as described earlier, American assets become more attractive and British investors will invest in dollar-denominated assets. The lower British interest rate leads to an increase in the supply of pounds in the foreign exchange market. At the same time, American investors will find British assets less attractive and will decrease their demand pound-denominated assets and hence decrease their demand for pounds. This combination of an increase in supply and a decrease in demand for pounds creates a surplus of pounds and a pound depreciation. The pound depreciation will increase net exports, aggregate demand, and GDP. This effect complements the increase in aggregate demand due to the increase in investment, making monetary policy more effective than fiscal policy in stimulating aggregate demand and GDP.

Let us now summarize the effects of monetary and fiscal policies on the current account. An expansionary monetary policy leads to a depreciation of the currency and an increase in the current account. On the other hand, an expansionary fiscal policy leads to a currency appreciation and a decrease in the current account.

Macroeconomic Policy under Different Exchange Rate Systems

We have already analyzed the effects of monetary and fiscal policies under a floating exchange rate regime, where the government permits the exchange rate of its currency to freely change or float based on changes in the supply and demand for the currency in the foreign exchange market. Some countries maintain a fixed exchange rate regime, where the government sets a fixed exchange rate between its currency and another foreign currency. Under this regime, the government would create a fund of foreign currency reserves to intervene in the foreign exchange market to maintain the fixed value of the currency.

Monetary and Fiscal Policies under Fixed Exchange Rates

Suppose the British pound is fixed to the dollar and the Bank of England decides to increase the money supply. The increase in the supply of money leads to a decrease in British interest rates relative to American interest rates, which puts pressure on the pound to depreciate. To prevent the pound from depreciating, the Bank of England will then intervene in the foreign exchange to increase the demand for pounds by buying pounds and selling dollars. Foreign exchange brokers and banks will purchase the dollars by reducing their pound bank accounts and bank reserves. This sale of dollars is like an open market sale by the Bank of England, which results in a decrease in the British money supply. The foreign market intervention offsets the initial increase in the money supply, leading to no change in aggregate demand and output, thus making monetary policy ineffective under a fixed exchange rate regime.

As detailed earlier, an expansionary fiscal policy by the British government and the financing of the budget deficit lead to an increase in British interest rates. Higher British interest rates put pressure on the pound to appreciate. To prevent the pound from appreciating, the Bank of England must intervene in the foreign exchange market and buy dollars and sell pounds. The purchase of dollars in the foreign exchange market is similar to a domestic open market purchase of government bonds, which leads to an increase in the money supply and a decrease in interest rates. The decrease in interest rates will stimulate domestic investment, which complements the expansionary fiscal policy in increasing aggregate demand. Unlike monetary policy, fiscal policy is even more effective than under-floating exchange rates because the intervention prevents the currency from appreciating and making exports more expensive.

The Monetary Trilemma

We demonstrated that if a country chooses to fix its exchange rate, it cannot use monetary policy to affect aggregate demand and output. Thus, policy makers face a monetary trilemma in choosing the appropriate exchange rate regime to achieve their economic objectives. The trilemma refers to the impossibility of having all three of the following: (1) a fixed foreign exchange rate, (2) free international capital flows, and (3) the ability to pursue an independent monetary policy. According to the trilemma, a central bank can only follow two of the three policies. If it wants to pursue a fixed exchange rate policy and maintain free capital mobility, it must give up an independent monetary policy. If it wants to pursue a fixed exchange rate policy and an independent monetary policy, it must give up free capital mobility. If it wants to pursue an independent monetary policy and free capital mobility, then it must give up a fixed exchange rate policy and let the currency float. The United States has free capital mobility, and the Federal Reserve conducts an independent monetary policy, which explains why the dollar floats in the foreign exchange market. For many years, the central bank of China pursued an independent monetary policy and fixed the value of the yuan to the dollar. To do so, it placed severe restrictions on international capital flows.

The Bretton Woods System of fixed exchange rates put strict limits on capital movements, thus permitting countries to have some degree of independence for monetary policy to pursue internal balance. On the other hand, for many years, China fixed the value of yuan to the dollar and could pursue an independent monetary policy by severely limiting capital flows.

The Choice of an Exchange Rate System

According to the International Monetary Fund (IMF), of the 189 member countries, around 37 percent permit their currencies to float, and the remaining countries have some form of a fixed exchange arrangement. The IMF classifies the exchange rate regimes based on the actual practices followed by its members. These include hard pegs, where the currency of another country is the legal tender of the country, such as Ecuador, which uses the U.S dollar. Hard pegs also take the form of a currency board, where a foreign currency backs the quantity of the domestic money. The U.S. dollar backs the Hong Kong dollar. Soft pegs are various forms of fixed or pegged exchange rate regimes. Under a conventional fixed peg, the currency is allowed to change within a margin of ± 1 percent of the par value. Under the horizontal band, the currency fluctuates within a margin of more than ± 1 percent of the par value. There is also a crawling peg, where the currency is allowed to change within a ± 1 percent, but the par value is changed periodically, and finally, there is a crawling band, where the currency changes in a band of more than ± 1 percent of the par value and the par is changed periodically.

Under a freely floating regime, a country allows its exchange rate to change according to the changes in the supply and demand for the currency. Under a managed floating regime, a country's monetary authority may intervene in the foreign exchange market to manage the float.

Despite the various forms of exchange rate regimes, studies have shown that the performance of an economy does not depend on the choice of fixed versus floating rates but on the economic characteristics of the country such as, the size of the GDP, the degree of openness, the inflation rate, and the concentration of trade. Large economies are less inclined to give up their domestic economic policies and goals to maintain a fixed exchange rate. Large countries also tend to be relatively closed economies, which means their net exports are a small part of their GDP. The more open an economy is, the greater the impact of exchange rate changes on their international trade and hence the more significant the impact on their GDP. Thus, closed economies will opt for flexible rates, and open economies will favor fixed rates. Open economies whose trade is with primarily one major country tend to maintain a fixed rate with their major trading partner, while countries with a diversified set of trading partners will favor floating rates.[1]

---

[1]H. Edison and M. Melvin. 1990. "The Determination and Implications of the Choice of an Exchange Rate System." In W. Haraf, and T. Willett, ed. *Monetary Policy for a Volatile Global Economy* (Washington, D.C.: American Enterprise Institute).

CHAPTER 11

A Brief History of International Monetary Systems

The Gold Standard

From 1880 until 1914, the global economy operated under an international monetary system known as the gold standard. Under this system, the amount of gold and currency in a country represented the supply of money, and each country set the value of its currency in terms of gold, known as the mint parity. For example, the Bank of England set the mint parity of the pound at £20 per ounce of gold, and the U.S. Treasury set the mint parity of the dollar at $40 per ounce of gold. Then the exchange rate of the pound relative to the dollar was set at two dollars per pound. There were no formal agreements between countries, but each country tried to maintain the mint parity by offering to buy and sell gold for domestic currency in unlimited amounts. For example, suppose Britain ran a current account deficit with the United States, which put pressure on the pound to depreciate. To prevent this depreciation, the Bank of England could sell its gold reserves in exchange for pounds. This sale of gold reserves gives people gold in order to buy dollars. Since dollars and gold could be exchanged for one another, an increase in the supply of gold was the same as an increase in the supply of dollars. As a result, gold would leave Britain, reducing the British money supply, and enter the United States, raising the American money supply. The decrease in the British money supply would then lead to a decrease in the British price level, and the increase in the United States money supply would lead to an increase in the American price level. These would make British goods more price competitive, leading to rising exports and declining imports and reducing British net exports.

With the beginning of World War I, many countries began to focus on building armies and navies. Most governments borrowed money to pay for the war and the reconstruction after the war. All countries except for the United States abandoned the gold standard and allowed their currencies to float. After the war, some countries reestablished a partial gold standard but with exchange rates that were unsustainable. Germany suffered from very high rates of inflation, and Britain experienced negative economic growth and high unemployment. The gold standard collapsed in the middle of the Great Depression as countries tried to revive their economies by restricting trade and devaluing their currencies.

The Bretton Woods System

In 1944, 44 countries met in a hotel in Bretton Woods, a small town, in the state of New Hampshire in the United States, to create a new international monetary system, which became known as the Bretton Woods System. The Bretton Woods System created two new international organizations: the International Monetary Fund (IMF) and the International Bank for Reconstruction and Development, also known as the World Bank. The World Bank's purpose was to provide loans and technical assistance to low-income countries and to promote economic development. The purpose of the IMF was to promote exchange rate stability and an open system of international payments. Under the Articles of Agreement of the IMF, each country agreed to fix or peg the value of its currency to the dollar. In turn, the United States agreed to fix the value of the dollar to gold at a rate of $35 per ounce of gold. The currency pegs were to remain fixed except when a country faced a fundamental balance of payments disequilibrium, where it experienced a prolonged period of large balance of payments deficits or surpluses. The IMF is like a central bankers' bank. A country had to contribute reserves, called the country's quota, in the form of gold and other currencies as a condition for joining the IMF. If a member experiences a balance of payments problem, it can borrow funds from the IMF. The country purchases international reserves from the IMF using its domestic currency reserves. The country then is obligated to repay the IMF by repurchasing its domestic currency reserves with its international reserves. In 1969 the IMF created the Special Drawings Right

(SDR), an international reserve to add to the existing member countries' official reserves. SDRs are allocated based on a country's IMF quota. The SDR is neither a currency nor a claim on the IMF but serves as a unit of account of the IMF and some other international organizations. IMF members can use their SDR quotas to obtain currencies from other members to settle their imbalances. The value of the SDR was equivalent to 0.888671 grams of fine gold—which, at the time, was also equivalent to one U.S. dollar. After the end of the Bretton Woods System in 1973, the SDR's value is based on a basket of currencies. Effective October 1, 2016, the SDR basket consists of the U.S. dollar, the euro, the renminbi, the yen, and the pound.

The U.S. dollar played a significant role in the Bretton Woods System. While other countries pegged their currencies to the dollar, the United States was not responsible for pegging the dollar. Its primary obligation was to hold the price of gold at $35 per ounce and stood ready to exchange foreign government dollar holdings into gold. Other central banks continued to hold dollars, being confident in their ability to convert their dollar reserves into gold.

After World War II the United States had current account surpluses with many countries and held about two-thirds of the world gold stock. Over time, the United States began to run current account deficits, which led to continued increases in foreign dollar holdings. By 1965, the total amount of foreign dollar holdings exceeded the U.S. stock of gold, and foreign governments began to lose confidence in the convertibility of their dollar holdings into gold. Many countries began to demand gold for their dollar holdings. Facing a gold shortage, the United States changed the value of the gold to $38 per ounce, effectively devaluing the dollar, and finally, in 1971, the United States suspended its commitment to buy and sell dollars for gold. The United States, Britain, and other countries moved to a floating exchange rate system.

The Euro

Another significant change in the international monetary system occurred in 1979 when the governments of the European Economic Community established the European Exchange Monetary System, which established a system of fixed exchange rates among themselves. A key feature of this system was the creation of the European Currency Unit (ECU). The value of the ECU was a weighted average of member currencies, and it was used as a unit of account. Central banks were committed to keeping the value of their respective currencies with respect to the ECU, and the ECU was allowed to float against the dollar.

In 1992, representatives from 12 countries—Belgium, Denmark, France, Germany, Greece, Ireland, Italy, Luxembourg, Netherlands, Portugal, Spain, and the United Kingdom—signed the Maastricht Treaty, which officially came into force on November 1, 1993. The Maastricht Treaty established the European Union (EU), the European Central Bank (ECB), and the European System of Central Banks, and created a single currency, the euro. The primary objective of the ECB is to maintain price stability and manage the value of the euro. If a country wished to join the euro, it had to meet specific criteria. First, its annual government budget deficit cannot exceed 3 percent of its GDP. Second, its public debt must be under 60 percent of its GDP. Third, it must keep the value of its currency fixed to the euro for at least 3 years. Fourth, its annual inflation rate must be within 1.5 percent of the three EU countries with the lowest inflation rate. Fifth, its long-term interest rates must be within 2 percent of the three lowest interest rates in the EU.

The United Kingdom and Denmark met all the criteria but decided not to use the euro and are not required to be a part of the Eurozone. Austria, Finland, and Sweden became members of the EU, although Sweden has not adopted the euro. Slovenia was the first former socialist country to adopt the euro, followed by Slovakia, Estonia, Latvia, Malta, Cyprus, and Estonia. Bulgaria, the Czech Republic, Hungary, Poland, Croatia, and Romania belong to the EU but do not currently meet the criteria for joining the Eurozone.

The euro is the currency of an area with a GDP of over $12 trillion. The euro has been around for twenty years and it's exchange rate has been quite volatile. Its most severe test occurred during the financial crisis of 2008 and the Greek debt crisis.

CHAPTER 12

International Banking and International Capital Markets

It is essential for corporate financial managers of multinational companies to understand the various international sources of funding that are available through international banks and international capital markets. Multinational corporations can use their own funds or raise funds in the international capital markets by issuing stocks, selling bonds, or borrowing from banks either domestically or internationally. The main actors in the international capital markets include banks, corporations, nonbank financial institutions (insurance companies, mutual funds, hedge, pension funds), central banks, and other government institutions. Commercial banks are the most important actors in the market because they facilitate trade in goods and services and engage in a wide range of international activities. Nonbank financial institutions have moved into the international capital market to diversify their asset portfolios and to underwrite the sale of stocks and bonds by corporations. Central banks are involved in foreign exchange intervention, and other government institutions sometimes borrow from other countries. The most important international financial centers are London, Tokyo, and New York. Some smaller economies like Switzerland, Luxembourg, Hong Kong, and the Bahamas also serve as important world financial centers.

The International Bond Market

An international bond is issued by a company in a currency other than the company's currency. The first international bond was issued in 1963 by an Italian company and was denominated in U.S. dollars. These bonds became the world's first *eurobonds* since they were issued in Italy and denominated in U.S. dollars rather than Italian lira. From the perspective of a domestic investor and resident of the United States, an international bond is one that is issued by corporations or governments in other countries denominated in a currency other than the U.S. dollar.

Eurobonds are different from foreign bonds. A *foreign bond* is a bond where a foreign company issues bond denominated in the currency denomination of the foreign country. For example, a U.S. company issues a bond and raises capital in Mexico denominated in Mexican peso. Foreign bonds have interesting names, such as a *Yankee bonds*, which are bonds issued by a foreign company or bank that is denominated in dollars and traded in the United States bond market; *Samurai bonds*, which are yen-denominated bonds issued by non-Japanese firms in the Japanese bond market; and *Bulldog bonds*, which are pound-denominated bonds issued by non-British firms in the British bond market.

All foreign bonds must be registered and are subject to the rules and regulation of the foreign country where these bonds are issued. For example, Yankee bonds have to be registered with Securities and Exchange Commission of the United States and have to follow the same requirements of domestic bonds. All foreign bonds are also rated by credit-rating organizations. Unlike foreign bonds, eurobonds are not governed by any official agency or regulator.

Since international bonds are typically denominated and pay interest in the currency of the host or domestic country, the value of the bond in the domestic currency will fluctuate depending on changes and exchange rates between the domestic country and foreign country. These bonds are, therefore, subject to currency risk.

International Banking

Many domestic banks also engage in international banking activities. A domestic bank may establish a *correspondent* relationship with a local bank in another country to conduct trade financing, foreign exchange services, and other services to its customers. A domestic bank may establish a *foreign branch*, which would then operate as a regular bank in the foreign country and is under the rules and regulations of both countries. Unlike a foreign branch, a *subsidiary bank* is wholly or partly owned by the bank, but it is incorporated in the foreign country and is subject to the banking rules and regulations of the foreign country but not the parent bank's country.

An *offshore banking center* is a center where a bank lends and borrows to nonresidents of the country, and the transactions are initiated outside of the center. Offshore banking centers also offer low or zero taxation, very little regulation, and secrecy. Offshore banking centers are found in the Bahamas, Bermuda, the Cayman Islands, Hong Kong, Panama, and Singapore.

Edge Act banks are subsidiaries of U.S. banks that are in the United States but are permitted to engage in a full range of international banking activities, such as accepting deposits from foreigner customers, transferring international funds, and trade financing. A U.S. chartered bank can operate an international banking facility.

In addition to offshore banking, there is a large volume of offshore currency trading. An offshore deposit is a bank account denominated in a currency other than that of the country where the bank is located. For example, a dollar deposit in a Swiss bank is called a Eurodollar. The creation of Eurodollars started after World War II when the United States sent millions of dollars to Europe to help with the reconstruction of the countries devastated by the war. Some foreign countries, including the former Soviet Union, also had deposits in U.S. dollars in American banks. Following the Soviet Union's occupation of Hungary in 1956, the Soviet Union decided to move its dollar deposits in American banks to a Russian bank in London which had a British charter for fear of its assets being frozen by the United States in retaliation for the occupation.

There are three types of transactions in the Eurodollar market. One transaction happens between two non-U.S. residents. For example, a French resident deposits dollars in a British bank, which, in turn, lends the funds to a Canadian company. Another type happens between two U.S. residents. For example, a U.S. resident deposits dollar in a Cayman Island branch of a U.S. bank and the U.S. bank located in the United States borrows the money from its branch. The third type is between a U.S. resident and a non-U.S. resident when the parties borrow and lend from another across borders. It is difficult to estimate the size of the Eurodollar market since banks are not subject to any rules or regulations of the host countries, but it is well over $5 trillion. The major reason for the growth of the Eurodollar market is the difference in national bank regulations and taxes. London, which has fewer banking regulations on foreign denominated deposits, has become the center of the Eurodollar market.

The International Equity Market

A multinational company can also raise funds by issuing shares in its home country's stock market or can cross-list their stocks in foreign stock markets. Cross-listed stocks are traded in the form of a depository receipt, which is a number of shares held in custody by a bank in the country of the stock exchange. When foreign companies list their stocks in the United States, they usually use American depository receipts which are held in banks like the Bank of New York Melon, JPMorgan Chase, and Citigroup. There are also global deposit receipts, which can be traded on many stock exchanges, and there are global registered shares that are simultaneously traded in many markets in different currencies.

Unlike the international bond market, there is no such thing as a global equity market. International equity markets are not as developed or uniform as the bond markets. Most of the corporate stocks are traded in the domestic stock markets, with its own set of rules and regulations for listing shares and investor protections. If a company wants to raise funds abroad, it must choose a specific country and a specific exchange and a type of security. In general, the costs are often higher than for a domestic issue.

CHAPTER 13

Epilogue

This book has aimed to provide a brief guide to international economics for business students and corporate managers. The study of international economics is more vital today than in previous times. After decades of trade liberalization, countries have become more protectionist. The issues of jobs, intellectual property protection, barriers to trade in services, access to domestic markets, immigration, and currency manipulation have again emerged as major economic and political issues. Many countries have engaged in negotiating trade agreements on a bilateral or regional basis rather than multilateral negotiations under the WTO. The United States has imposed tariffs on a range of finished products and intermediate inputs from China, Canada, Mexico, and the European Union. In turn, these nations have retaliated by levying their tariffs on American goods. The United States withdrew from the Trans-Pacific Partnership Trade Agreement and renegotiated the NAFTA, renaming it the United States-Mexico-Canada Agreement. Another significant development is Brexit, the United Kingdom's vote to withdraw from the European Union.

Parts I and II of the book focused on international trade theory and policy. Chapter 2 examined the pattern of trade based on the theory of comparative advantage and factor endowments and the effects of trade on the distribution of income. Chapter 3 introduced new trade theories that integrated the role of firms in international trade. The effects of tariffs and other trade instruments were covered in Chapter 4. A tariff can be placed on an imported finished product or an intermediate good. The objective of a tariff on a finished imported good is to protect the domestic industry by increasing the price of the imported product. This is different if a tariff is levied on an imported input used by a domestic company, which then increases the costs of production, putting the company and the industry at a competitive disadvantage at home and abroad.

A tariff can shift production away from the country that is protecting its domestic firms when other countries retaliate and levy tariffs of their own on the final product. For example, when the European Union placed a duty on Harley Davidson, in retaliation to the tariffs set by the United States on European steel and aluminum, the company decided to move production to other countries to avoid the European Union tariffs. The rise of global value chains means that any tariffs implemented by a single country or sector will likely affect other regions and sectors. Tariffs by the United States and China are likely to affect companies in Vietnam, Malaysia, or other countries that are part of the global value chain. This makes the job of multinational corporate managers more complicated as they must assess the short-run and long-run effects of tariffs on their overall operating and corporate strategies.

Chapter 5 examined the arguments for trade protectionism and the political economy of trade policy. Companies, industry associations, and unions spend millions of dollars to influence lawmakers responsible for passing trade legislation. Corporations must analyze the effects of proposed trade policies on their costs and revenues to lobby for or against the policies. Chapter 6 introduced the World Trade Organization and trade issues. The WTO's Doha round of negotiations failed due to disagreements over agricultural subsidies and intellectual property rights. There are no rules or agreements on digital trade, services trade, and *trade in* products that can help achieve environmental and climate protection goals.

Parts III and IV of the book focused on international finance and open economy macroeconomics. It explained the foreign exchange market and the determination of exchange rates in the short run and the long run. Exchange rate changes affect the operating profits of companies in globally competitive industries and domestic companies that have no foreign operations or exports but face significant foreign competition in their home market. While changes in the exchange rate are beyond the control of corporate managers, there are strategies that managers can implement to manage exchange rate risks. But more importantly, it is vital for managers to understand the underlying causes of changes in the exchange rates both in the short run and in the long run to be able to be proactive rather than reactive to exchange rate fluctuations. For example, managers must pay attention to changes in a country's monetary policy that affect interest rates and hence the exchange rate. They must also be aware of a country's rate of economic growth and inflation rate and their effects on the long-run exchange rate.

The last chapter briefly described the international capital markets and the role of banks in the global economy. Companies can raise funds by issuing stocks or bonds in domestic markets or foreign markets. Another option for companies is to obtain loans from commercial banks. Corporate financial managers must then weigh the costs and benefits of each financing option.

For the past 30 years, "globalization," defined as the international flow of goods, money, and people, has steadily increased, yet this trend has slowed down recently. Trade and capital flows as a percentage of world GDP have decreased and the capacity of supply chains that ship intermediate goods has decreased.

Part of this decline was due to the financial crisis and the Great Recession of 2008–2009. The United States, the European Union countries, Japan, China, and other industrialized nations experienced a decline in exports and imports.

Services are becoming a major sector of most industrialized nations. Unlike trade in goods, many services are more difficult to trade due to domestic legal and licensing restrictions. While the export of services has not grown over the past decade, e-commerce has been growing. Companies like Alibaba, Netflix, and Facebook have millions of international customers. Technology services are also subject to protectionism and politics. The United States discourages Chinese technology companies from operating in the country, and Facebook and Twitter cannot operate in China. India does not allow Walmart and Amazon to own inventories in India to protect its domestic retailers.

Emerging economies are going beyond being locations to assemble intermediate products to producing the intermediate inputs. Multinational companies must reevaluate their supply-chain activities, and some are exploring ways to shift production from China to other countries. Furthermore, the share of cross-border supply-chain foreign inputs that are from the same region is rising.

The dollar is still the world's dominant currency, and the decisions of the Federal Reserve on interest rates influence interest rates and exchange rates in other countries. Yet the United States is losing its dominance in the global economy. China has replaced the United States as the major trading partner of many countries, and changes in Chinese GDP affect the exports of these nations. China has embarked on a massive program of infrastructure development known as the Belt Road Initiative by assisting Asian countries in building roads, ports, and bridge to connect it to Europe. It is possible that in the foreseeable the future, the Chinese currency may challenge the dollar in the global financial system.

References

Bank for International Settlements. *Triennial Central Bank Survey of Foreign Exchange and OTC Derivatives Markets in 2016.* https://www.bis.org/publ/rpfx16.htm (accessed February 24, 2018)

Broda, C. and D. Weinstein. May, 2006. "Globalization and the Gains from Variety." *Quarterly Journal of Economics* 121, no. 2, pp. 541–85.

Boulanger, P. and P. Jomini. 2010. "Of the Benefits to the EU of Removing the Common Agricultural Policy," *Sciences Politique Policy Brief.*

Bureau of Economic Analysis. "International Transactions, International Services, and International Investment Position Tables," *International Data.* https://apps.bea.gov/iTable/iTable.cfm?ReqID=62&step=1 (accessed January 6, 2018)

Dewey, C. June 8, 2017. "Why Americans Pay More for Sugar," *The Washington Post.* https://www.washingtonpost.com/news/wonk/wp/2017/06/08/why-americans-pay-more-for-sugar/?utm_term=.ca56b4eab528 (accessed August 9, 2017)

Edison, H. and M. Melvin. 1990. "The Determination and Implications of the Choice of an Exchange Rate System." In *Monetary Policy for a Volatile Global Economy*, ed. W. Haraf and T. Willett. Washington, D.C.: American Enterprise Institute.

Euromoney. May 30, 2018. *Euromoney FX Survey 2018—Press Release.* https://www.euromoney.com/article/b18f5s6kqtcr6m/euromoney-fx-survey-2018-press-release?copyrightInfo=true (accessed February 24, 2018)

European Commission. *Promotion and Distribution of European Works.* https://ec.europa.eu/digital-single-market/en/promotion-and-distribution-european-works (accessed January 30, 2018)

Feenstra, R.C. and A.M. Taylor. 2017. *International Economics.* New York: Worth Publishers.

Helpman, E. Spring, 1999. "The Structure of Foreign Trade." *Journal of Economic Perspectives* 13, no. 2, pp. 121–44.

Irwin, D.A. 1996. *Against the Tide: An Intellectual History of Free Trade.* Princeton: Princeton University Press.

Johnston, M. "How New York Became the Center of American Finance," *Investopedia.* http://www.investopedia.com/articles/investing/022516/how-new-york-became-center-american-finance.asp#ixzz4nI8Tdis6 (accessed July 16, 2017)

Krugman, P. May, 1983m. "New Theories of Trade among Industrial Countries." *American Economic Review* 73, no. 2, pp. 343–47.

Krugman, P. 1996. "A Country Is Not a Company." *Harvard Business Review*, January-February Issue, pp. 40–51.

Pendle, G. 2015. "Dalton, GA: How a Bedspread Fiefdom Became a Carpet Kingdom." *Atlas Obscura*. https://www.atlasobscura.com/articles/from-the-bedspread-capital-of-the-world-to-the-carpet-capital-of-the-world (accessed July 15, 2017)

Ricardo, D. 1957. *On the Principles of Political Economy and Taxation*, London: J.M. Dent & Sons.

Smith, A. 1937. *An Inquiry into the Nature and Causes of the Wealth of Nations*. New York: The Modern Library/Random House.

Stolper, W.F. and P.A Samuelson. November, 1941. "Protection and Real Wages." *The Review of Economic Studies* 9, no. 1, pp. 58–73.

Trade Partnership WorldWide. *The Unintended Consequences of U.S. Steel Import Tariffs: A Quantification of the Impact during 2002 (2003)*. http://tradepartnership.com/reports/the-unintended-consequences-of-u-s-steel-import-tariffs-a-quantification-of-the-impact-during-2002-2003/ (accessed October 5, 2017)

United States Department of Commerce. *Fact Sheet: Section 232 Investigation on the Effect of Imports of Steel on U.S. National Security*. https://www.commerce.gov/news/fact-sheets/2017/04/fact-sheet-section-232-investigations-effect-imports-national-security (accessed January 14, 2018)

United States International Trade Commission. *Official Harmonized Tariff Schedule 2018*. https://www.usitc.gov/tata/hts/index.htm (accessed September 23, 2017)

World Trade Organization. *Dispute Settlement*. https://www.wto.org/english/tratop_e/dispu_e/dispu_e.htm (accessed October 25, 2017)

World Trade Organization. *European Communities and Certain Member States— Measures Affecting Trade in Large Civil Aircraft*. https://www.wto.org/english/tratop_e/dispu_e/cases_e/ds316_e.htm (accessed November 26, 2017)

World Trade Organization. *Intellectual Property: Protection and Enforcement*. https://www.wto.org/english/thewto_e/whatis_e/tif_e/agrm7_e.htm (accessed December 5, 2017)

World Trade Organization. *Technical Barriers to Trade*. https://www.wto.org/english/tratop_e/tbt_e/tbt_e.htm (accessed September 24, 2017)

World Trade Organization. *The General Agreement on Trade in Services (GATS): Objectives, Coverage and Disciplines*. https://www.wto.org/english/tratop_e/serv_e/gatsqa_e.htm (accessed November 24, 2017)

World Trade Organization. *World Trade Statistical Review, 2016*. https://www.wto.org/english/res_e/statis_e/wts2016_e/wts16_toc_e.htm (accessed June 21, 2017)

About the Author

Shahruz Mohtadi is a faculty member at Hult International Business School, and at Suffolk University, Boston, MA. He has over 35 years of experience teaching international economics to undergraduate and graduate students and author of articles in academic journals and books. He earned a BS in international trade and finance and a PhD and MS in economics from Louisiana State University, Baton Rouge, LA.

In today's global economy, it is vital for corporate managers to have a fundamental knowledge of international trade and finance. How does your company compete with foreign companies that have lower labor costs? What are the effects of a tariff on your company, and how should you deal with its effects? How can you protect your company's intellectual property? How do changes in currency exchange rates affect your company, and how to manage exchange rate risk? In a nontechnical way, this book explains why countries trade and the role of firms in global trade and describes the effect of tariffs and other barriers to trade on a company's sales, costs, and profits. Also, the book explains why exchange rates fluctuate and the effects of exchange rate changes on a company's bottom line.

Index

OTHER TITLES FROM THE ECONOMICS AND PUBLIC POLICY COLLECTION

Philip Romero, The University of Oregon and
Jeffrey Edwards, North Carolina A&T State University, *Editors*

- *A Primer on Microeconomics, Second Edition, Volume II: Competition and Constraints* by Thomas M. Beveridge
- *A Primer on Microeconomics, Second Edition, Volume I: Fundamentals of Exchange* by Thomas M. Beveridge
- *A Primer on Macroeconomics, Second Edition, Volume II: Policies and Perspectives* by Thomas M. Beveridge
- *A Primer on Macroeconomics, Second Edition, Volume I: Elements and Principles* by Thomas M. Beveridge
- *Macroeconomics, Second Edition, Volume I* by David G. Tuerck
- *Macroeconomics, Second Edition, Volume II* by David G. Tuerck
- *Economic Renaissance In the Age of Artificial Intelligence* by Apek Mulay
- *Disaster Risk Management: Case Studies in South Asian Countries* by Huong Ha, R. Lalitha S. Fernando, and Sanjeev Kumar Mahajan
- *The Option Strategy Desk Reference: An Essential Reference for Option Traders* by Russell A. Stultz
- *Disaster Risk Management in Agriculture: Case Studies in South Asian Countries* by Huong Ha, Lalitha S. Fernando and Sanjeev Kumar Mahajan
- *Understanding Demonetization in India: A Deft Stroke of Economic Policy* by Shrawan Kumar Singh
- *Urban Development 2120* by Peter Nelson
- *Foreign Direct Investment* by Leena Kaushal

Announcing the Business Expert Press Digital Library

Concise e-books business students need for classroom and research

This book can also be purchased in an e-book collection by your library as

- *a one-time purchase,*
- *that is owned forever,*
- *allows for simultaneous readers,*
- *has no restrictions on printing, and*
- *can be downloaded as PDFs from within the library community.*

Our digital library collections are a great solution to beat the rising cost of textbooks. E-books can be loaded into their course management systems or onto students' e-book readers. The **Business Expert Press** digital libraries are very affordable, with no obligation to buy in future years. For more information, please visit **www.businessexpertpress.com/librarians**. To set up a trial in the United States, please email **sales@businessexpertpress.com**.

www.ingramcontent.com/pod-product-compliance
Lightning Source LLC
Chambersburg PA
CBHW061326220326
41599CB00026B/5050